Musing and Munching

Musing and Munching

A Memoir and Cookbook

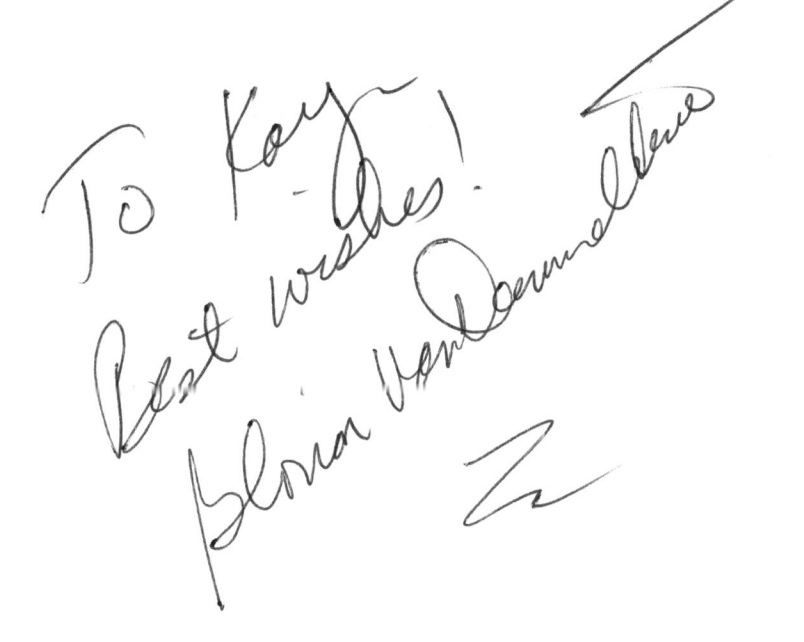

To Kay—
Best wishes!
Gloria VanDemmeltraadt

Gloria VanDemmeltraadt

Copyright © 2009 by Gloria VanDemmeltraadt.

Library of Congress Control Number: 2009912536
ISBN: Hardcover   978-1-4500-0144-1
             Softcover   978-1-4500-0143-4

All rights reserved. No part of this book may be reproduced or transmitted in any form or by any means, electronic or mechanical, including photocopying, recording, or by any information storage and retrieval system, without permission in writing from the copyright owner.

This book was printed in the United States of America.

To order additional copies of this book, contact:
Xlibris Corporation
1-888-795-4274
www.Xlibris.com
Orders@Xlibris.com

Contents

Hello 7
Chapter 1 The early years 9
Chapter 2 On my own 25
Chapter 3 Gene 30
Chapter 4 The farm 47
Chapter 5 After the farm 65
Chapter 6 The end and the beginning 76
Chapter 7 Travels 86
Chapter 8 Thanks for our blessings 104

Recipes (with separate table of contents)

Breakfast 117
Appetizers 123
Main Dishes—Entrees 128
Soups 150
Vegetables, Sauces, and Salads 157
Desserts 167
Drinks 182
Fun Stuff: Notes, reminders, interesting stuff, and doo dads 183

Hello

Sometimes it seems that by experiences and bumps in the road that some of us live more than our years would allow. Such is the case for me, a 68 year old gray-haired grandma, who's survived a whole bunch of life-style extremes and is still managing to ride the bumps and smile through it all.

Memories are like sifting flour. The original product is one thing, and when it is sifted or strained through a screen it falls below in a new form. Memories are sifted through the minds of everyone who shares the same event, and the resulting product is changed forever. Each of us, through our unique makeup and set of experiences, captures and remembers a different version or translation of the same event. For this reason, I ask for thoughtful understanding of family and friends in my interpretation of events that they may have shared.

My children have been urging me for a long time to document some of my life encounters, but it just never seemed to come together in the right way. I've tried to journal dozens of times, but have never kept it up more than a few days at most. Sadly, I've just forgotten or put aside many important events for which I would now love to have a record. An example would be all of the events I've sung for through the years, including literally hundreds of weddings, funerals, political events, singing telegrams, plays, nightclub shows, church services, and more. Why I didn't simply write down or make a list for all of them is distressing. When the children of couples for whose weddings I sang 30 plus years before began to call, I had no record of when or what I sang for their parents, and memories are pretty dim also.

I have friends who document everything and have albums of pictures and writings organized chronologically or some such logical way. Not me. I have unlabeled boxes, bags, and drawers full of pictures scattered everywhere, and no writings at all, to speak of. Somehow, the living of my life seemed more important, and surely more fun, than organizing it.

Recently, because of new experiences with foods and menus, the thought came that I could record some of my background while overlapping it with the far-reaching variety of foods that have followed my life's path.

In addition to wanting me to write down the stories of my life, my children have long been asking me to write down some of the recipes for foods they liked while growing up. I was reluctant to do it because I've always been one to use whatever is on hand, and throw in a handful of this and that. Every dish was different every time I made it so I never gave them any recipes.

I've chosen to put this book together by telling some of the significant stories of my life and emphasizing them with recipes and menus that may have played a role in those stories. Many of the recipes are my own, but most have been gathered from friends and other sources from all over the world.

My heartfelt thanks go to all of the folks from far and near for sharing the recipes that are printed here. Lots of them were written on scraps of greasy paper or napkins with ingredients but no directions, and that makes them even more precious.

Let's see how it goes . . .

Chapter 1

The early years

In the tiny town of Hadley, Minnesota in the troubled year of 1941, my mother sprawled on a board between two chairs to give birth so that she wouldn't make a mess. Such was my dramatic if ignoble entrance into the world.

In equally dramatic fashion, I was named Gloria after the glamorous and impressive actress Gloria Swanson, a striking presence of the day.

My parents, Janet and Joseph Everett Tyler (Everett to his parents and Joe to everyone else) and my older sister and brother, lived on "the farm" along with and owned by Everett's parents. Everett was always the favored son. Tall, handsome and charming, he was a crowd-pleasing baseball player. Everett also had a wild streak and loved to frequent dance halls where shameless "flappers" boogied in joyous abandon to raucous and boisterous music. In 1930 Janet was such a flapper and the sister of his friend as well, who encouraged Everett to go to "the Cities" (as Minneapolis and St. Paul are still called) and meet this striking girl. Everett was captivated at first sight by Janet's alluring and joyful spirit. Though three years older than he, she must have been equally charmed, as their hastily planned wedding followed in short order.

Everett moved his young bride to the farm with his parents, and unfortunately, Everett's mother was not so captivated. Life must have been difficult at best for my Mom to live with this disapproving mother-in-law, which she did for the next dozen years. But life went on with farm chores, gardens, baseball games, and the births of my sister Frances, and brother Neil.

Of course, I don't remember any of this or what life was really like on the farm, except for a couple of comments my Mom made about those years. She told me that she once hid a dish that had cracked in the dishpan because she feared the lecture and screaming that she would get from her mother-in-law.

Janet loved to read but reading was considered laziness, so some days she would sneak out an upstairs window after her chores were done and sit on the porch roof to get a few minutes alone to read.

However, she was not one to ever complain and little Frances was the image of Grandma Tyler and much adored. Then Neil arrived and was as handsome and outgoing as his father. My birth was another story—I looked just like Janet and some years later prompted a nasty comment from my Grandmother, "Isn't it a pity that poor little Gloria is so homely!"

1. Frances, age 12 with baby Gloria

When I was about two years old, Everett's father died. The farm was sold and my parents eventually came to live in Hopkins, Minnesota. My dad worked for a steel company and then the County, grading and plowing roads. When my little brother Bucky (okay, that's Bruce to everybody else) was born, Mom went to work as a fry cook in a tavern, and whatever good cooking she might have done on the farm was surely undone by the influence of the tavern, I suspect. Simply put, childhood memories of meals are not the best. Gritty lettuce from the garden, overcooked colorless vegetables floating in water, and hard-as-a-rock fried pork chops. We had rutabaga stew that smelled as it sounds. However, what she lacked in cooking skills, Mom made up for in her baking. Throughout her lifetime, she made bread and pies that were without equal. In later years, she would visit us and bake bread every day, filling the freezer with crusty loaves that we enjoyed for weeks. Bucky's favorite, lemon meringue pie, was divine.

Recipes: (Desserts) Pie Crust
Recipes: (Desserts) Lemon Meringue Pie

The onset of several nasty childhood illnesses like mumps, measles, and whooping cough all at the same time, sapped my physical strength, and I developed double pneumonia at age eight. I very nearly died. I remember going to Abbott hospital lying in Mother's lap because I couldn't stand up. I was there for a couple of weeks and came home in a wheel chair, still so weak that I couldn't walk for quite a while. I was thin and anemic and needed iron for many years to build up my blood.

The good news was that massive doses of newly discovered penicillin saved my life, but it was also decided that in order to keep that life, I needed enriching goat's milk to boost my strength. The bad news was that my parents had no way to get goat's milk, and even providing the supervision that an ailing child needed was out of reach at that time. However it happened, family came to the rescue and without warning, Bucky and I were whisked off to Nebraska the moment school was out.

Dad's older sister Florence and her husband Joe lived on a farm outside the tiny town of Diller, Nebraska, population 180. In addition to cows and horses and pigs, they had a milk-goat that was waiting just for me. First appearing stern and serious, Aunt Florence was a little frightening in the beginning, and the fact that Grandma Tyler lived with them was even scarier. I didn't spend much time in the house.

I spent my days with Uncle Joe, riding on his tractor, "helping" with farm chores, and mainly getting in his way, I'm sure. And, yes, I milked the goat, with Uncle Joe's help, of course. The worst part was that little Bucky was told that he had to hold the goat while I milked it. Only four years old that summer when I was almost nine, Bucky dreaded that chore more than words could say. Finally, Grandma Tyler told him that he had to hold the goat or go to bed without any supper. Not saying a word, Bucky went upstairs to bed at 3:00 in the afternoon.

Somehow we both survived that summer. I became stronger and Bucky learned to hold the goat. I also began a lifelong love for our aunt and uncle, and we spent more joyous summers with them while growing up. What we ate there besides goat milk puddings, I cannot remember, except that once in a while we went to town for free movies in the park and ice cream cones.

I suspect that the key reason we went to Nebraska for many summers was that our parents couldn't afford to keep us at home or provide anyone to watch us. Sometimes they drove us there—it was 500 miles to Diller—but once we rode with some neighbors who were taking a trip to the Southwest. They were in a hurry and apparently not very happy to have two extra little kids along. They dropped us off on a street corner in Lincoln and didn't wait for anyone to pick us up. We stood there quite a while before Uncle Joe and Aunt Florence found us, and a relieved and happy reunion it was.

At home in Hopkins, I was beyond shy to the point of fearful for most of my childhood years. Searching memories, I try to determine why I spent a period of time unable to speak out loud to adults, a couple of years at least. Surely, therapists would have a field day with that one. I truly don't know whether a specific dark incident happened that I've cut out of my memory, or if it was an accumulation of fears that caused it. There were many fears.

My friend Jan and I would go to the corner store if we each had a nickel, and she would ask the man for two mint candy bars because I wasn't able to ask him myself. Jan was sort of a bully and she made fun of me for having freckles, being skinny, and not being able to talk to grown-ups. But I was desperate for a friend and I liked being around her perfect family. Sadly, I was used to being told that I was ugly and hopeless, so Jan's comments weren't anything new. I hung around her house as much as I could where there was a mom who made cookies and a dad who came home every night and spent time with the family.

My dad went to Archie's. Mom worked pretty much around the clock in those days, so he would steal away to his favorite bar for as many beers as he could hold, and charm the ladies. I remember overhearing phone calls urging him to come home, and at least once I was sent downtown to bring him home. That didn't work and I was propped up at the bar with a soda, a rare treat, while I waited for him to finish entertaining whoever was on his arm.

I learned many years later that there were several serious incidents including one where he ran off with a girlfriend to California, or toward that direction, before sobering up and calling Mom to come get him. She always bailed him out, and never a word was said about it. None of us knew about these events until many years after his death.

After the pneumonia I was forced to wear somebody's castoff "rubbers" to school to keep my feet dry. The other kids wore boots and nice footwear, but my rubbers were big and floppy and really ugly. They invited much pointing and giggling, and I was totally humiliated. One time at school when others laughed as I came into the classroom, I stayed the whole day hiding in the coat closet alongside my rubbers, refusing to come out. I slunk down in the corner and stayed there. The teacher tried to coax me to come out, and of course, I wouldn't talk to her. There was an opening at the bottom of the closet door about six inches high, and at the end of the day, I handed the coats and boots and belongings of the other children through the opening. When everyone was gone, I crept out and went home.

My parents were working long hours and Frances and Neil had their own teenage lives. To this day I have no idea where Bucky was or who took care of him when he was small. Our Mother's memoirs say that she went to work at the tavern when Bucky was three weeks old and she worked nights until he was four. She said that Neil was supposed to watch the baby. Neil was 12 at the time, so it's anybody's guess as to how much care the baby got, and I fended for myself.

Times were different then. Today this would be called child abuse, and maybe it was. The sad truth is that I pretty much grew up like a weed, untended and neglected for more than several years. But life was tough, and "daycare" wasn't an option in those days. My Mother had a handsome and charming, but drinking and philandering husband and a houseful of kids. She did what she had to do to survive.

Years later, at her home in Diller when she was well into her 80's, Mom approached this subject and it's the only time she ever did. In her business-like and matter-of-fact way—to keep from crying, I believe—she let me know that she knew how neglected I had been as a young child. She said, "I'm so sorry for all of the things that happened to you when you were little, and I wish that things could have been different." Then, in her inimitable, pragmatic way that anyone who knew her would expect, she immediately said, "Now, how about a game of Scrabble?"

There was significant age difference between the four of us kids: Frances was born in 1930, Neil in 1934, I in 1941, and Bruce in 1946. The older ones were rarely home and I still don't know where the baby was during my grade-school years.

I spent a lot of time alone and came home after school most days to an empty house. Terrified, I would quietly open the storm door into what was called, "the back entry." The ice box was there and the room was small and crowded with boots and coats and dusty stuff, with no place to sit or to hide. I listened carefully at the door to the house. If all was quiet, I'd slowly open the door and creep softly past the dreaded basement door and through the kitchen into the dining room. I squeezed behind the china cabinet where I could see but not be seen. I stood there in the corner afraid to make a peep and disturb the monster that lurked in the basement. Sometimes it was hours until someone else came home.

I became friends with all of the precious things in the china cabinet. My mind's eye saw my grandfather drinking hot coffee out of the mustache cup, its little ledge keeping his bushy mustache dry. I imagined colorful flowers in the dark blue vase, or sipping some mysterious tea out of the delicate translucent cup that I would never dare to touch.

Mom used to make sauerkraut in the basement. She put it in huge crocks under the steps and as it fermented, it bubbled and gurgled and actually moved. The frightening noises convinced me that this stuff was alive! Seeing as how the basement also held the dreadful washing machine with the arm-grabbing roller bar, as well as the black-hole-from-hell, the coal room, it was a fearsome place. One time, my brother Neil, in a teenage moment, locked me in the basement and turned off the light. He thought it was funny, but my screams and wet pants were long remembered. To this day, I am leery of basements, and being in a dark room alone still throws me into panic.

Life wasn't all bad through my early years. My sister Fran was a beacon of hope. Eleven years older than I, she was the most beautiful and accomplished person in my world. She graduated high school, had boyfriends, competed in the Hopkins Raspberry Queen contest, moved with a girlfriend to Chicago to work, and most of all, she didn't think I was ugly! When others teased me about my freckles, she explained that I was special and the little spots were really angel kisses. Oh joy!

Frannie once took me with her to Chicago to stay at her apartment during a school vacation. I went to work with her at a furniture store for a couple of days and thought I was in heaven. She arranged for a photograph to be taken of me, and I could hardly believe that sophisticated, smiling girl was me. What a glamorous life she had, in my 12-year old eyes, and she became my role model for life.

2. Gloria, age 12

I have to add that somehow after those early years of little supervision and care, my parents arranged for me to have piano lessons for a few years—from Sister Arthur at the Catholic church, and that's another scary story. I even (reluctantly) learned to play the accordion. My suspicion is that the pneumonia illness scared everybody enough that someone decided this kid needed some attention. Anyway, life got better after that, and even though I wet the bed for years and never did get over my fear of the dark, I quit hiding under chairs and behind the china closet and slowly began to be a real person.

My father was extremely prejudiced against Catholics—and pretty much anyone else who didn't look and believe just like he did—but Catholics were scary! On the rare times that we (not Dad, but everyone else) went to church, it was the Lutheran church we went to even though my mother proclaimed herself a Methodist until she died. Catholics on the other hand, did secret things that even Dad couldn't talk about, but he warned us to *never* associate with a Catholic.

There was a Catholic family down the street from our house. They looked pretty normal, but I knew there was some hidden strangeness that I couldn't understand. I was afraid to walk on that side of the street when going by, and would cross the street when passing their house, just in case.

When I was informed that I would be taking piano lessons, I was scared enough, but when I learned that my teacher would be a Catholic Nun, I thought for sure the end was coming. Sister Arthur looked like her name sounded; large, serious, and lipless. She wore the old-style long black habit with a huge and heavy cross hanging around what must have been her neck. She had no neck or feet or teeth that I could see. She glided in and out of rooms, and never once did I see her smile or even look pleasant.

Those lessons lasted at least a couple of years, and I don't remember ever uttering a single word to Sister Arthur. I crept silently into her studio, a tiny room buried in the bowels of the cold stone edifice of the Hopkins Catholic church. I perched on her piano bench, feet dangling. When I proved to be an unwilling learner, she demanded that I come every day after school for weeks to write notes on the blackboard. If I played a wrong note during my lessons, she hit my fingers with a wooden ruler.

The edict was that I would learn to play a piece called "Falling Waters," for my father. He said that when I learned that song I could quit piano lessons. I worked doggedly at what must have been a beautiful piece, but it was agony for me. The day finally came and I remember playing the dreaded song at the old upright in our dining room. My parents were sitting stiffly at the table, listening carefully to each note as my fingers flew over the ivory keys, some of them ivory-less. Finally it was done. I closed my eyes and held my breath, to silence. Suddenly Dad applauded, hollered, "Good job!" and that was the end of my piano lessons.

Tom and Anna lived next door. Anna used to make Bohemian prune-filled pastries that my parents loved, but I was so afraid of Anna that I never ate them. Here is an essay that I once wrote from scary childhood memories about Anna.

Anna

Blue sky. That's what I saw when the sweet rush of summer air filled my aching lungs and woke me, lying there on the hard packed dirt. And then I remembered—Anna! I turned my head with a painful jerk, and there she was. Watching me. She had never moved from her spot on the worn wooden bench under the apple tree in her yard that was next to mine. She saw me fall. She saw my swaggering run and the daredevil jump up to the clothesline pole to hang by my knees, showing off for all the world. And she didn't move to help when I fell, even seeing me lying there unconscious with the very breath knocked out of me.

I was ten that summer when I learned what cruelty was. It was then I knew it was true, what Tom had said. I believed that Anna really had killed two husbands.

Anna was always there, silent and disapproving of the world. She grimly did the chores that came with a house and a big garden and some chickens, and never ever smiled or even acknowledged the children next door. The other kids would giggle and run away when she glared at us with her dark and joyless eyes, and ageless, wrinkled face. But I was shy and never dared to make much noise around Anna.

Her husband, Tom, was a big gentle Irishman with smile lines all over and boot blacking on his eyebrows. He was always telling stories and I listened in awe to every one. There were stories of Ireland, the most perfect place on earth, and stories about his two strapping sons. I always wondered what strapping meant, but it sounded wonderful.

The story I remember the most was about Anna's husbands. Tom insisted that Anna had killed two husbands before him and he'd be damned if she was going to kill him. He said she ran over the first husband with a wagon. I never did find out for sure what happened to the second, but it must have been grisly the way Tom carried on about it.

Anna kept a grey striped barn cat, simply called "Cat." Cat lived in Anna's barn and ate mice and chased the rats away from the chickens. Sometimes Cat would sneak away next door and curl up in my lap if I was really still. She felt warm and prickly soft, but she didn't like people much and never stayed long.

Anna didn't want the kittens that Cat would produce every now and then, so she drowned them. She didn't do it when they were brand new and sightless. No, she waited till they were cute and furry and tumbling all over each other and Cat was having trouble keeping them together. With my little brother and me clutching the wire fence on our side, wide eyed and terrified, but still watching, Anna stuffed all the kittens one by one, in a grungy old gunny sack. Then she filled a big bucket with water, sat in the middle of her yard, and dunked that sack. She had to hold it down in the water because the kittens were crying and bumping around in the sack. Soon they were quiet.

We didn't feel much like playing after that. I think my little brother went to bed. I sat on the step a while and thought about the second husband. I knew then what happened to him.

One morning Anna didn't come out to do her chores. There was a lot of fuss next door with people coming and going, and some men in a big black car came and took Anna away. Funny, she made such a tiny lump under the sheet when they carried the stretcher out of the house. How could all that meanness hide in that tiny lump?

My Dad laughed because Tom finally got his wish; he outlived Anna. I was glad for Tom, too, because he was going to live with the strapping sons, and stories or not, I knew she *really* killed those husbands.

Recipes: (Desserts) Prune Kolaches

3. Gloria the acrobat, in a happy moment

Northfield

The summer I turned 15, Bucky and I were again in Nebraska with our relatives. This trip we were allowed to visit some cousins who lived on another farm near our Uncle Joe. I learned to ride horses there and envied my bold cousins who rode rodeo-style going at break-neck speed and doing daring tricks. Grandma Tyler disapproved of all of those cousins and was not happy at all for us to be there. We stayed with that family for part of the summer and chopped thistles out of the cornfields for hours each day. At night we would go home to plates heaped with crisp fresh corn—and nothing else—for supper.

We played in the barn and would climb high in the rafters, swing from a thick rope and drop into the hay squealing with delight. On one round of swinging on the rope, my hands loosened and I slid down the rope, my hands rubbing over several big knots, burning all the way. I landed in a heap of pain with several fingers burned and torn. Needless to say, that was the end of the adventure with our cousins and it was back to Uncle Joe's and Grandma Tyler. I stood with bandaged hands and head hanging in her dark and cheerless room while she railed about how stupid I was. Her room smelled like the chamber pot kept under her bed, and she never opened the curtains, which added to the gloom. I closed my ears to her ranting and fled as soon as possible.

At the end of summer Mom wrote that we wouldn't be going back to our home in Hopkins. It had been sold and they were making plans to move. My parents were active in the Odd Fellows Lodge, and Dad had taken a new job in Northfield, Minnesota. He was to manage the old people's home that was sponsored by the Lodge, and we would be living there. Whoa—an *old people's home*—how could they?

Ninth grade in Hopkins had been a pivotal year for me. At the beginning of the year, I resisted in tears when my little group of girlfriends started walking the wrong way down a one-way alley. I was afraid of doing something that I knew was wrong and terrified that we might get arrested. Patiently, they convinced me that *walking* the wrong way was okay. Then, instead of pushing me away, they stayed friends with me. What joy was mine!

Also that year, I took Latin from a wonderful teacher who instilled in me a life-long love of ancient Rome and Greece. She encouraged me more than any teacher I ever had, and taught me how to study. I began to think that maybe I wasn't so stupid after all.

I was 15 years old that summer and finally realizing that I could maybe become a real person if I really tried. I was to enter tenth grade at Hopkins High School in the fall and was envisioning making more friends and doing whatever it was that teenagers did. Now, everything was changed and I'd be moving to a small town and living in an old people's home? I was devastated!

Originally, the Odd Fellows Home in Northfield had been an orphanage, and through the years had moved from young to elder care. There were still four children living there, and Mom informed us that we would be living together with them. More bad news!

Bucky got the worst of it—Dad had a large dormitory built in the huge old building that housed our apartment, and Bucky shared the dormitory with the three boys. The one girl had a private room next to mine. There were some other staff living in part of the building and the administrative offices were there, but there was another building for residents, as well as a nursing home structure.

The other children were siblings and except for the girl, we got along fine. The poor young girl had many problems and one day tried to set our building on fire. This did not go well with the Fire Marshall, and Kay was moved away that very day. The boys soon followed and as it turned out, their parents were still living in the area, though divorced, and the young people went to live with one or the other of them. We kept track of each other for a while and I had a huge crush on the oldest boy, but our lives went on in different ways.

Meanwhile, we not only survived, we thrived at the Odd Fellows Home. I was more than nervous about going to a new school, and that first day was frightening. But, after some good experiences the year before, and knowing that there was nothing I could do to change the fact that we were moving, I had made a remarkable personal determination. I resolved that starting this new stage of my life, I would *not* be shy or scared anymore as I had been for most of my life. Could I do it? Only time would tell.

Mom urged me to audition for the high school chorus, which I saw as a first step, and I did it. Not realizing at first that it was a real triumph to be invited to sing with this special choir, I was pleased and a little scared when I heard that I passed the audition. Once there, our director, Yosh Murakami, made me sing a song alone in front of the choir—a roomful of strangers. Hoping for the floor to open up and swallow me, I sang the song. There was silence and then to my great shock, applause. Yosh then took me under his wing and this kind and understanding man gave me private lessons all through high school. This caring act launched a lifetime of singing and love of music, and changed my life forever.

After school I worked in the big dining room of the Home. I helped to serve dinner to the residents—good, balanced food, if bland and a little soft. We ate there, too, at a separate table for our family, and after dinner I set the tables in the big dining room for the next day. I loved to walk through the huge kitchen where the cooks, Nelson and Corrie, reigned supreme. There were wonderful smells, rolling steam from the dishwashers, and always a special treat for me along with strict discipline, too.

Recipe: (Desserts) Chocolate Cherry Bars and Chocolate Chip Oatmeal Bars

I walked back to our apartment after work through the underground tunnel from the "new building," where the residents lived, to "Forest Hall," where we lived. To get to the tunnel, I had to pass the pool room where the resident men played pocket pool. Many evenings they invited me for a quick game and I became pretty adept with a pool cue.

I spent time with my girlfriends and way too much time with my boyfriend. In hindsight, which we all know is 20-20, I let myself be led by my boyfriend, and made some bad choices, particularly in not studying enough. I could have won scholarships if I had applied myself, but I didn't listen to my teachers. We didn't have counselors then, and my parents were too busy with their own lives to watch mine close enough.

Northfield was a small town with a malt shop downtown, exactly like the current parodies of the '50's. We wore sweaters and poodle skirts, drank cherry cokes and ate hamburgers at the malt shop, and the girls were forbidden to enter the door of Tiny's, the local smoke shop. We had slumber parties at each others' houses. When it was my turn I invited all of the girls in my class. Most of them came if only to see where I lived that would accommodate such a number. Living in an old people's home was pretty unique, and our living room, which was a former gathering place for the residents, was enormous. At the evening's end there were at least 30 bodies lolling on blankets and sleeping bags throughout the room, whispering and giggling.

We danced at Caper Club, a weekly event for teens, where the girls lined up on one wall, and the boys on another. Mostly the girls danced with each other, and a few couples joined in. We all knew every word to every song. One time, I went with a bunch of girls to "the Cities," to see Dick Clark, who came to Lake Calhoun in Minneapolis. We screamed and bounced and danced to the music, convinced that life didn't get any better than this.

I spent three years at the Odd Fellows Home, and have to say that I never resented not living in a "normal" house through high school as my friends did. I learned a lot from the residents and from my experiences with them. I sang for their special parties and loved to hear their life stories that they were eager to tell. They especially loved to hear me sing the old Irish songs, like "My Wild Irish Rose," "Danny Boy," and others. I helped my mom with Bingo sessions and other game playing events.

One consequence of having our meals prepared for us was that my mother did no cooking during those years, nor did she teach me to cook. She worked long days as Matron of the Home, which meant she did all of the office work, planned activities for residents, supervised pretty much everything, and tried to keep my Dad in line. He had an eye for the pretty nurses. Unfortunately, it didn't stop there.

One evening in early spring prior to my high school graduation, Mom asked me to come to her room for a "chat." More than unusual, this was a first. Chatting was something that we just didn't do in our disconnected lives at the Home.

I crept into her room in great apprehension. She told me that things were not good with their marriage and that there might be a divorce. I was shocked as she continued to say that she might be living alone and would have all she could do to take care of Bucky. She said that my boyfriend Jerry wanted to marry me and if I would do that, then she wouldn't have to worry about me. I was completely surprised by this and didn't know what else to do except what she had advised. I talked with Jerry later, and we decided to get married right after I turned 18.

As things developed, my parents did not divorce. They left the Odd Fellows Home soon after my wedding, and bought a tavern in Savage, Minnesota. The tavern years were very hard, and I know they and Bucky suffered, but Mom was determined to stay with Dad. She cooked at the tavern and they lived in a dismal and ramshackle rented house. I worried a lot about Bucky and if we had had room, would have brought him to live with Jerry and me. However, from later discussions with Bucky, he never really minded those years and seemed to do well in school. I believe that he was a good and necessary presence in our parents' lives in those hard times.

Eventually, Dad gave up drinking, how or why I never knew, but it totally changed their lives. They sold the tavern, moved to Burnsville and Dad worked for the high school as a janitor and school bus driver. Amazingly, he turned out to be the most loved bus driver of all time in that area and was several times featured in local papers along with his dog, Tiny. Mom did office work and they were very happy in their later years.

Looking back, again with 20-20 hindsight, I felt safe with Jerry and thought that he "would take care of me," as Mom had hoped. I loved Jerry's family. He had a "real" Mom and Dad who stayed home and took care of their family. They lived in a big old comfortable house in the country on a small acreage. Hazel cooked and gardened, and also had a job in town. They were quiet and kind, and very good to me.

In September 1959, Jerry Shigley and I were married at St. John's Lutheran Church in Northfield. The reception was held at the Odd Fellows Home and the residents were thrilled to be part of our wedding. Jerry had worked there, too, as a night watchman, so many of them knew him.

So—I'm 18 years old and married. Now what? I didn't know how to cook, didn't know how to clean or do laundry, or pretty much anything. Everything was done for me at the Home, including cleaning my room. I just put my dirty clothes outside my door into a basket and they reappeared clean and folded. I did learn to sew and spent the summer after graduation making my wedding dress. But aside from being able to set a table and serve bowls of food cooked by somebody else, I knew absolutely nothing about how to keep a house or cook meals.

We bought a tiny trailer house and for a time, lived at the trailer court in Northfield. Before long, Jerry's parents, Hazel and Lloyd, gave us a small piece of land near their house on which to put our 30 x 8 foot trailer. We somehow survived 2 years in it, eating fish sticks and broccoli, which was all I could cook.

4. Gloria actually cooking (or pretending to) in 1959

One winter our water line, which was a buried hose from Jerry's parents' house next door, froze. For three months, I carried from their house every drop of water we used. I never forgot that winter, and to this day, I never waste water.

When baby Paul Allan was born in June 1961, we bought a bigger trailer and stayed in the same place. Mark Gerald came soon afterwards in October 1962. Jerry was working for Schjeldahl, an up and coming plastics company, and I was doing office work at Carleton college. During these years, Hazel was trying her best to teach me to cook. She made wonderful Norwegian delicacies.

I mainly watched and ate the results of her labors, but I did learn to make some of them, too.

Recipe: (Desserts) Rosettes, Fattigmand, Lefse, Sandbakkels, Krumkake

I also learned to make Hazel's toffee bars—a recipe that is still a favorite with anyone who tries them.

Recipe: (Desserts) Toffee Bars

Hazel also made the dreaded, stinky lutefisk, which she served on Christmas Eve. My Dad loved it, and our families spent several Christmases together at the Shigley's with bountiful tables.

We decided to build a house on the land that Jerry's parents had given us. This was a huge effort and expense, but with lots of help from neighbors, friends, and relatives, we put up a basement, got a pre-built frame, and almost finished the interior. I say almost, because before it was completely finished, Jerry decided that he didn't want to be married any more. In the late winter of 1966, he left me a note and moved to California with a girl from his workplace.

To everyone's surprise, especially mine, I discovered that I was pregnant, and Jerry's response was, "Well, that's *your* problem." Yes, it surely was.

As the saying goes..."Into each life some rain must fall." Well, it poured for quite a while.

Jerry's parents were embarrassed at what was happening with our disintegrating family, and they didn't want to stay in Northfield. They, too, pulled up stakes and moved to California, where they had another son and family. This was good for them, but it left the children and me even more on our own.

Here is a sad/funny piece that I once wrote about that time.

It

It was early fall; a lonely and frightening time for my two little boys and me. Their daddy had left us the winter before, before we even knew that I was pregnant. He said that he didn't want to be married anymore.

I don't remember much of spring or summer that year. It was more a matter of getting through it all. The new house in the country was sold, Daddy went to California with somebody else, hurts were hidden, and life went on. We ended up in a dreary apartment above somebody's house in town.

We sat outside on the steps a lot. Just being together, those two little scared-faced boys and me. I worked in an office and they went to a sitter all day, so our short time at night was special. We prayed a lot that Daddy would come back.

I've often wondered about those prayers. Sometime later I met a woman whose husband was dying. She was torn between praying that he would die and be at peace, or that he would live and not leave her. She was tormented by the struggle of what to pray for and her agony was painful to see. Finally, a kind person suggested that she pray for herself instead, to give her the strength to accept whatever happened. This simple suggestion changed everything. The terrible weight went off her and she bore the coming days with a wonderful peace.

I had no such kind friend at that time and kept on praying for my husband's return. He did not come back and our lives spiraled down in miserable suffering.

Finally, in the fall, my beautiful little girl was born. In true miracle fashion, though a painful and scary time it was, I brought home a healthy, happy little sister, for two, not much older, but world-wise big brothers. From the start she belonged to them. And they all belonged to me.

It wasn't easy, of course. Just getting through the chores involved with a job, a car, an apartment, and four people kept us all running. It was hard to remember that they were children, and tiny ones at that, as much as I expected of them.

One morning in the midst of the normal rush the baby fell over and bumped her head. Paul said Mark pushed her. I started yelling at Mark to say he was sorry, all the while dashing around bundling everyone up in scarves and mittens and mufflers, making them into three little "doughboys" to meet the cold outside the door. I repeated again and again, "Say it—go on, say it! Aren't you sorry you hurt your little sister?"

How cruel I was. That confused little four year old boy was terrified of his mother at that moment, but determined to do what was expected. I ranted on, "Say it!" Finally, just as we were ready to pile in the car, Mark looked up at me with fear widened eyes, hoping against hope that he was doing the right thing and said in a tiny voice, "It."

When I realized what he tried to do and what he really said, all the anger and hurt and exasperation of months of fear and anxiety came pouring out in my tears and laughter, and theirs.

We never went to work that day. We sat on the step and watched the leaves and hugged each other. We sang songs and laughed, and hugged each other some more. And we didn't pray again for Daddy to come home.

Chapter 2

On my own

I was working in the business office at Carleton College, in Northfield, but I needed more money to support my family. Soon after Karen was born in September 1966, I took a job at the bank downtown as an insurance secretary. I also worked in a pizza shop a few nights a week. The bank president didn't think it was "seemly" for bank employees to "moonlight" in a pizza shop. He was an odd man who walked around the bank picking his nose and watching us work. When he came near my area, his nose picking would get frenzied and he would walk by and glare at me several times a day.

St. Cloud

Bucky was going to college in St. Cloud and when he heard that I was on my own, he suggested that I move there with the children and live with him. He believed that my chances of succeeding alone were not good in the small community of Northfield. We envisioned me going to college in St. Cloud as well as working, and the two of us sharing living expenses. Brave or stupid, I decided that this might work and took the plunge.

I made some phone calls and set up an interview with a prominent insurance company in St. Cloud, and took a day off to go talk with them. Gullible and naïve, I was lured to a position that sounded ideal by a man whom I should have known was looking for more than an office worker. After talking about the job at his office, he invited me to dinner, where he glossed the possibilities with potential advancements, promotions, and dollars. With stars in my eyes, I took the job, eager to start a new life.

Excited and ambitious, I went back home and gave notice on both my jobs. With the help of friends, we packed up our meager belongings over a weekend and moved to St. Cloud, almost a hundred miles away. Bucky had rented an old rickety house that seemed to fit all of us, and I found a babysitter who would take all three children. We got things put away and settled in the old house, with a lot of scrubbing to help the drab and decrepit state of it.

Monday morning brought me fresh and ready to learn a new work world, and I opened the door to the office where I had been hired. A hard-faced woman said she had bad news; there had been a mistake and there was no job for me. The man who had offered me the moon was out of town and was so sorry, yada yada.

Stunned and frantic, I stumbled out the door and tried to gather my thoughts. What would I do? I couldn't go back to Northfield—I had quit my jobs and given up my apartment. We were here in this new town where I knew nobody. My children were relying on me—how would I start the search for work here?

In 1967 there were no cell phones, but there were phone booths on almost every corner downtown. I found one that had a phone book and started through the yellow pages. I focused on insurance agencies and began making the rounds to sell myself. I *had* to have a job—*immediately*!

After a long day of disappointing news including a session at the local employment agency, I was told that there was no one in town who needed someone of my skills at that time. I insisted that there must be someone out there, and after much prodding, a woman at the employment agency told me about Wally Honer. She said that he had hired someone recently who didn't work out and maybe if I checked with him, he might know of someone who could help me. It was the end of the day and I was out of options, so I went quickly to this man's office.

Wally was a long-time business man, an insurance/real estate guy who knew everyone and was a true St. Cloud "local." After I truthfully told him my story, he said that he knew and didn't like the man who had said he would hire me. Then he surprised me by saying that even though he really didn't need anyone right now, he would give me the chance to prove myself, and could I start the next day.

Staggered, but grateful and hopeful, I did start work the next day. I was determined to prove my worth and very shortly became an integral part of Wally's business. True to his word, Wally appreciated my good work and I stayed with the Honer Agency for more than three years.

The living situation with Bucky didn't last long. The drafty old house ate up our heating dollars quickly, and he couldn't handle little Karen bouncing on his head in the early morning in her very wet diapers, hollering her first word: "Bucky, Bucky!" He also was embarrassed when somebody from the church left a "care package," at Thanksgiving time. But he ate the food along with the rest of us—we needed it. Before long, he went to Mexico to do his student teaching and we gave up the house.

After that things got really financially tight, and my dad insisted that the children and I move back to Burnsville with them and live in their basement. I couldn't imagine a worse fate.

Dad had always been larger than life. Everything he did was over the top. He didn't talk, he yelled. He didn't stand, he towered, he didn't laugh, he bellowed. When he drank, he couldn't stop until he passed out. And when he finally did quit drinking, he got a ridiculously tiny dog on which he lavished all of the affection and love and kindness that he'd withheld from his family for more years than I want to remember.

Even though this was in Dad's post-drinking era, he was a huge man, tall and heavy, and my children were terrified of him. The little dog, named Tiny, rode around on his shoulder. Tiny adored Dad but snarled and snapped at everyone else, including Mom. Dad never understood why others didn't love Tiny as he did.

5. Taken in 1968, Janet and Joe Tyler with Paul, Mark, and Karen, plus Tiny who does not look happy.

We would visit Mom and Dad often. I know that Dad loved the children and me in his way, but the kids were never comfortable with the yelling or the dog. In addition, Dad insisted on calling Karen's dolly "Esterbeullah," which he thought was funny but it made her cry. These visits were tense and didn't last long, but Mom did her best, and we went home with bags full of canned goods to sustain us until the next visit.

Wally Honer came through again and let me cheaply rent a basement house that he owned. He didn't want to lose me in his insurance office but couldn't give me more money, so he let me have the basement house for the taxes it cost; $40 a month. I liked my work in Wally's office, and was also taking a morning class at St. Cloud State University, voice lessons at noon, and soon started working nights at the restaurant/bar where Bucky worked to make ends meet. Whew!

To get the night job, Bucky told the owner that I was an experienced bar waitress. The truth was that I had never had a drink in my life and didn't know anything whatsoever about liquor.

I showed up for work in the mini-skirt and boots that my brother said I needed and proceeded to look around the dark room. How would I see to write anything down? Bucky told me that if I never wrote anything down I would learn to just remember what people wanted and he as bartender, would tell me what the costs were. The first night was scary but people were understanding and I muddled through.

The worst part came when with both hands I clutched a tray holding a "Singapore Sling" in a tall narrow glass. It looked like a big glass straw. Carefully making my way to a table in the corner, I tripped over a stool hidden in the dark bar, and literally threw the drink all over a woman's fur coat. More bad news/good news. The boss was standing in the doorway and saw me trip. He also saw that the woman was not the wife of the man she was accompanying. After much embarrassment on all sides, the incident was quickly dismissed and by some miracle unknown to me, I kept the job. Bucky said it was the mini-skirt.

Mini-skirt or not, by the end of the week I was flitting all around the room in utter determination. I had a tray balanced on the palm of my hand and I remembered what every person in the room drank. As I got more comfortable, I began to sing with Sharon, the piano bar player, and it wasn't long before customers would rather hear me sing "The Impossible Dream," and get their own drinks.

The nightclub job lasted for more than two years with me working at least three nights a week until 2:00 a.m. or so, and each day we were up early to start over again. (Truth be known, I hope I never hear "The Impossible Dream" song again.)

How I did all that makes me tired to think about now, but I was young. I needed to feed my kids and hoped that someday I could get educated enough to do it with only one job. We struggled on.

One day, the roof fell in—literally. While I was away during the day, neighbor kids played on the roof of the basement house we lived in, and this caused rips that let rain slowly collect in the ceiling. Luckily it was a Saturday morning when I was home, that the ceiling gave way. The tiles fell down and gallons of water came pouring down in my living room. I was drenched while trying to hold the tiles up enough to keep the water from pouring on the precious piano that Mom had given me. I looked at the mess and decided that crying wouldn't help anything.

I marched across the street to some newer apartments that I had heard about and banged on somebody's door. God led me to the right door because they helped me call the right people. We met the requirements for limited income and number of people in the family and two days later we moved to a beautiful three bedroom townhouse with subsidized rent. Off we went again.

We ate a lot of hamburger in those days—and Mom and Dad came regularly with more canned goods. To our delight, we had a basement in the townhouse with our own washer and dryer and a place for the kids to play. There was a field behind the house where the boys caught lots of snakes and lizards and creepy things, and several times I had to chase their dirty jeans across the basement floor because the pockets were filled with frogs.

One day we made a quick stop at the grocery store in the rush between jobs. We ate a fast supper and as I was leaving for the night job, I couldn't find my car keys. I had the children helping me search through the house with no luck and I was getting frenzied. Paul anxiously came to me and said, "I can't find the car keys, Mom, but did you know that the milk is on your dresser?" Sure enough, the keys were in the refrigerator.

Chapter 3

Gene

Life Gets Better

After four years of struggling alone to keep my children fed, clothed, and housed, and wondering if this was how it would always be, along came Gene Cannon. We met in July 1969 when I sang for the wedding of our friends Sharon the piano player, and Steve, the bartender.

Gene's wife, Dee, had died in a car crash the year before and he had two teenagers. He met my three lively children and fell in love immediately with little blond curly-haired Karen. By the end of August we both knew that this relationship could be permanent.

Some say that there's no such thing as a coincidence—that everything is meant to be. A saying goes that a coincidence is really God's way of choosing to remain anonymous. Coincidence or God's prodding, there's a curious story about my meeting Gene Cannon.

I was currently dating another man at that time whose name was Gene. And, he had a deceased wife whose name was Dee, and she had been killed in a car crash. Sadly, this Gene had a totally different attitude toward the memories of his wife and she became better in death than in life. What I mean is that in his eyes, she was so perfect that no one would ever be able to "compete" with her memory.

I knew that this connection would not become a good marriage for me because I would never be able to measure up to the standards that he was creating in his mind, and I was ready to end this relationship.

Sharon, my piano player friend from the nightclub where we both worked, knew about this situation, and she also knew Gene Cannon. She asked me to invite him to the wedding because he had given them a gift and she had forgotten to invite him. Surprising myself, I actually stood up the other Gene with whom I was already expected to attend the wedding, and went with Gene Cannon.

Years later, I heard from a friend that the other Gene never did marry. After his children grew up he became a sad and lonely old man who said in a Christmas letter, "I let all my chances go by."

My heart aches for people like him, who are so afraid to take a chance. They don't hear the quiet whisper of God who tries to guide us in the way we should go. Here is a story that exemplifies that very point. It also gives some good advice for men and the women who care about them. It's from a sermon that Gene Cannon gave in early 2002 about living under the shadow of death from the results of advanced prostate cancer. The sermon was titled, "Life is a Gift."

Listen for the Whisper

A proud young man was driving down a neighborhood street in his fancy new car. Suddenly, a brick smashed into the car's side door! He stopped, jumped out of the car, grabbed the kid standing there and shouted, "What do you think you're doing? The young boy said, "Please mister . . . please, I'm sorry. I didn't know what else to do," he pleaded. "I threw the brick because no one else would stop . . . It's my brother," he said. "He fell out of his wheelchair and I can't lift him up." Now sobbing, the boy asked the man, "Would you please help me get him back into his wheelchair? He's hurt and he's too heavy for me." The man lifted the handicapped boy back into the wheelchair, then took out his handkerchief and dabbed at the boy's scrapes and cuts.

"Thank you and may God bless you," the grateful child told the stranger. Too shook up for words, the man simply watched the little boy push his brother down the sidewalk.

The man never bothered to repair the damage to his car. He kept the dent there to remind him of this message: Don't go through life so fast that someone has to throw a brick at you to get your attention! God whispers in our souls and speaks to our hearts. Sometimes when we don't have time to listen, He has to throw a brick at us. It's our choice: Listen for the whisper . . . or wait for the brick!

I didn't hear the whisper . . . and man, did I get hit with a brick! Possibly, if we had known more about the simple blood test that can show if you have a prostate problem, I could have had more effective treatment in the beginning. But—maybe the brick hit *me* so I can share this message and save someone else. That message is; Men, if you're over 45 years old, get a PSA test *now*, and do it regularly for the rest of your life!

Back to 1969. After Sharon's wedding, Gene and I began seeing each other often. One evening Gene had just arrived at my house to take me out for dinner on my birthday. The babysitter was there, hugs and orders were given, and we were on the way out the door. Suddenly, my son Mark came screaming and bleeding, with a huge wound in his thigh. He had fallen from his bike and ripped open his leg by scraping against the pedal.

Instead of going to dinner, we spent the evening in the Emergency Room getting 27 stitches in Mark's leg. I told Gene that this was what life with me would be like and fully expected him to disappear, as had many before him.

Right after this event I was not feeling well and a nasty cold developed into pneumonia, my lifelong weakness. Unknown to Gene who had to leave town for a week for his work, I had to be hospitalized. My neighbor kept the children and I spent five lonely days worrying about how I was going to get well enough to go back to all my jobs and keep going.

In all of the trials and turmoils and events of my life, I believe that this week was the lowest point. I was barely able to keep a roof over our heads with my limited education, and now my health might be in jeopardy. Lying there alone in the hospital with scene after scene playing in my mind of how I would continue to take care of my children was greater than worrisome. It was more frightening than anything I had yet suffered through.

In my night job at the piano bar as a cocktail waitress, I had started singing more and more, at the urging of customers. They would rather listen to me sing and get their own drinks, and the tips were still there. I was urged by many to do more with singing, and maybe could have eventually succeeded with lots of help.

However, in my early investigating along those lines, I learned that any real hope for a singing career was impossible because of my responsibilities to the children. It wasn't that I resented that, but I learned too late that a life in the entertainment field has to be focused totally on the entertainer. There is almost no time or energy to do anything else in the life of a successful performer, especially one *seeking* to become successful, including having a family. It became clear that this was something I wasn't able or even wanting to do. There had to be another way for us to go on, but I was too mired in pain to see it.

Unknown to me, God had a plan for us. Not only did Gene not disappear, he returned from his trip, found out that I was ill and worked even harder to charm me by getting me checked out of the hospital and inviting me for a meal at his house which he cooked (turkey on the grill).

I met his children that day, Greg and Renee, ages 18 and 15. They were polite and well-mannered, and seemed willing to accept their father's choice. Needless to say, I was thrilled and decided that we just might be able to make this work.

After lots of discussion on all sides, my world-wise son Paul who was eight years old, met Gene at the door one evening and said, "Well, Gene, have you and Mom made the big decision?" We were married on December 27, 1969.

This story, written in 1998 for the Christ Lutheran Church Women's Faith Stories, tells about the beginning of our life together.

What Do We Do Now, Mom?

I looked down at the deep red carpet beneath my feet, slowly raised my eyes, and followed it forward. Who were all those people on the right? There they sat, stiff and formal, facing forward, with even the backs of their heads looking critical. I knew they were thinking, "For Heaven's sake, Gene, she's so young!" A stab of fear shot from behind my nervous eyes down to my already pinched but frozen feet, encased in their new, unbending, dyed-to-match shoes.

I shifted my gaze to the left. There was my friend, Faye. Her shoulders were shaking and she held a wadded up tissue to her mouth. Was she remembering the night we camped out in a cardboard refrigerator carton in her back yard and told scary stories all night? Or when we tried smoking in the alley by her house and I threw up? Oh, I wished we were still only twelve!

There was my little brother, Bucky, or Bruce, as he liked to be called, now that he was a college-man (he would always be Bucky to me). I remembered the afternoon when he was only five and I was ten, we went to a movie and stayed through the double feature three times (*The Black Stallion* and *Maggie & Jiggs*). When we came out of the theater it was dark and the police had been looking for us for hours. Boy, were we in trouble!

I shared a rented house with Bucky for a time after my divorce, when times were really tough. We were both trying to take college classes and work and keep my children fed. He worked nights in a bar and some nights he would bring home the leftover oranges, cherries and hunks of lime. We sat up late and ate this strange supper, imagining it was steak and laughing all the while.

I could feel my toes warming up. It was like the rich red carpet was full of memories and reaching up with its fiery color to thaw my fears. The warmth spread upward and out to my fingertips to meet the icy, slippery grips of two equally nervous young boys. They looked so much alike, these two blond haired, miniature men. The eight-year old a little taller than the seven-year old, both of them too responsible for their years. They looked at me with wide, apprehensive eyes and I could hear the question without words, "What do we do now, Mom?"

"What do we do now, Mom?" I heard that frightened and frightening question come from Paul, when his daddy left us almost four years before. I heard it from his brother, Mark, a few months later when their little sister was born. I heard it often during the hard times when they saw more of the babysitters than they did of me, and when we had to "stretch" the milk so they could all have some. And, I heard it from all of them when I told them that God had finally sent us a new dad.

This new dad was waiting for us at the front of the church. And with him were his children, ages 15 and 18. "Dear God—help me! What have I done?" I thought, "I'm only 28 years old, how can I know how to deal with teenagers? Their mother died. They could hate me for being alive, for bringing all these new mouths to feed, for taking their father's attention, for having to give up their rooms, and for a thousand other reasons."

In my panic, they all looked like strangers to me, including their father, and they looked back at us with solemn faces. Grim faces. Could it be that they were fearful, too? Were they wondering, too, who was this strange young woman with all those babies?

"How dare she try to take our mother's place. She'd better not try to make *me* babysit," I imagined his daughter thinking. Gene and I had only known each other for six months; maybe he was doubting his decision to take on all this new responsibility. Had we really thought honestly about the potential difficulties that could and would arise by joining together two unfamiliar adults and five children raised in completely different environments?

Second thoughts were becoming third thoughts, and we didn't move. The unsaid question hung in the air, "What do we do now, Mom?"

Suddenly the atmosphere changed. There was a sudden sound from the front of the church, and I began to hear polite chuckles from the congregation that grew to nervous giggles from some. In the wedding plan, my three-year-old Karen was supposed to walk quietly down the aisle with Gene's daughter Renee, and then sit with my parents for the rest of the service. However, she broke away from her new sister, ran through the church as fast as she could, hollered, "Hey Grandma!" and jumped in my mother's lap. In the silence right before the processional music started, Karen began crunching on the life-saver candy stashed in Mom's pockets. Her blond curls bounced as she laughed at everybody, and her open-mouthed crunching echoed through the sanctuary like amplified Rice Krispies in milk.

The stage was set, not just for this moment, but for the life that has followed as well. Laughter and the hand of God have shown us the way to raise and launch these five children plus one more. Laughter and God's love eased the way through sickness and health, through richer and poorer. More laughter has followed every tear, and loving prayer has made all of us feel cherished.

I tightened the hold on my little sons' hands, started down the aisle, and answered, "Come on boys, there's a new life waiting for us!"

6. The Cannon wedding, Dec. 27, 1969.
Front from left, Mark, Karen, Paul. Back, Greg, Gloria, Gene, Renee

There will be Little Children (tongue-in-cheek, by Renee)

After Dad asked Gloria to marry him, he started trying to prepare us for a life with little children in the house. After a while it began to seem like every little thing we did would provoke the warning, "Now, look. There are going to be little children coming into the house and things are going to have to change. I'm going to need your help to set a good example."

One fall day, Greg, Dad, and I went up to the lake. There were some things Dad wanted to do before it snowed. On our way back Dad said to me in the backseat, "Why don't you gimme one of those cookies back there." I responded, "Now, Dad, there are going to be little children coming into the house and you need to start setting an example. It should be *please* pass me one of those cookies." Dad looked at me for a full minute and then dryly said, "Gimme one of those &*%$ cookies before I break your neck." I quickly handed him the whole package and said, "That's much better!"

New Life

The new life was a struggle for all of us in the beginning, getting used to new people, new surroundings, and new foods. Greg and Renee were more accepting than I ever imagined. All of the children were polite to each other, which was nice to see, but not natural. The first time I heard one of the teens say, "Get out of here you little maggot!" I knew that they were finally blending as real brothers and sisters.

Being home during the day was a new experience for me and one that I loved getting used to after years of working two jobs at a time. I volunteered at the kids' schools, led the Cub Scouts and Brownies groups that the kids were in, and did the things that most Moms did. When an extra was needed for a baseball game, I filled in and we all had fun. One time Paul was talking about my playing ball with the kids and said something about ladies not doing that. I said, "But, Paul, I'm a lady, too." He said, "You're no lady, Mom, you're just a big girl!"

Lots of patience was needed, like the time that Karen sneaked into Renee's room and used her precious scented oils. Karen called them "perferumes," and came screaming down the stairs one day smelling sharply of cinnamon. She had smeared the oil on her cheeks and it was so strong that it burned her tender skin. She kept crying and saying, "I didn't do it, I didn't do it!"

Not long after Gene and I were married Bucky lived with us for a short time. He had come back from Mexico and decided he wanted to stay in the St. Cloud area. He didn't stay with us long and to everyone's delight soon married Cassandra, or Cassie, as we call her. Cassie was a teacher in the school that some of our kids attended, and she had a couple of them in her classes through the years. They and their son Nate have always remained close to our family.

Those early years were an adjustment for everyone, and then we learned that little Lee was on the way.

It happened that Gene was on a long and stressful trip out east, something that began with a steel hauler's strike where a couple of his company's trucks were being held up. He flew to Pennsylvania to negotiate with union officials. What I didn't know was that over the two weeks he was gone, he had several harrowing and stressful events happen to him.

First, he was threatened at gunpoint by strikers who were more than serious about keeping steel-hauling trucks from moving. After many discussions and much skillful negotiation, Gene was able to get his company's trucks released.

A few days later he was in Washington DC for a legal hearing. While he was walking alone on the street that evening, he was mugged by someone who sprang out of a doorway. He was hit in the face and lost his tooth, his diamond wedding ring and cash.

The next evening when he called home and had planned to tell me of his experiences, I didn't give him a chance to talk. I immediately burst out in tears and announced that I had found out that day that I was pregnant. The kids heard my blubbering conversation and came running. That led to lots of snuffling, lots of surprise, and no opportunity for him to tell me what had happened to him.

I never knew the real extent of these events until he told me about it years later. What I did know was that Gene came home from that trip without his tooth (broke it on a cookie at a truck stop café) without his wedding ring (left it in a restroom) and heavily smoking cigarettes after he had quit for more than a year.

I never had been much of a cook and suddenly I was preparing all meals for seven people. I was determined and the family was patient. Through lots of trial and error, I was eventually able to produce some edible meals for us. Gene traveled a great deal for his work, and when he came home he wanted simple food and loved my casseroles. I would put together any variety of noodles, soups, meats, and seasonings, and the family seemed to like it. Greg would say at least three times a week, "That's the best meal I ever had!"

Recipe: (Entrees) Tuna or Chicken Casserole, Hamburger Bake, Macaroni and Cheese

True to his Iowa roots, Gene liked everything creamed; vegetables, potatoes, even meat. He tired of steaks and chops that were standard fare for traveling folks, and loved my meat loaf. He would often get up at night and make a meatloaf sandwich.

Recipe: (Entrees) Meat Loaf (Basic), Meatballs, Creamed

We had a period of "ethnic dinners." Partly a ploy to get this diverse family together occasionally around the dinner table, we would have Italian night, or Chinese night or the like. I would fix appropriate food and everyone would dress in aprons, sarongs, kilts, tablecloths, baskets on their heads, you name it, and we would talk about the country or area while we ate. We also did fondue a few times, but sharp forks in young hands flinging hot grease around the room was more breath-holding than breath-taking. The ethnic dinners were fun but we ran out of ideas and they didn't last long. A couple of good recipes that came from that era were:

Recipe: (Entrees) Sweet and Sour Pork; Torsk (Norwegian Cod); Meatballs, Russian and Waikiki

With Gene traveling so much, the kids and I had lots of "popcorn" nights. These were nights that I didn't cook much except to feed the little kids. The older kids and I ate popcorn and I had my one drink of Scotch (very little Scotch and lots of water, but it was great). Renee and Greg and I would watch TV and hopefully a scary movie would be on. Later, Greg would make egg sandwiches for us—nummy!

Recipe: (Entrees) Egg Sandwich

Here's a cute story from Renee about what we called, "The Birthday Smear."

When Gloria and Dad got married we suddenly had lots of birthday celebrations. In the fall of the year it seemed as if we were having a birthday celebration every week. Gloria would bake a layer cake (we could pick what color cake and what color frosting we wanted). The first birthday we celebrated, someone said they got a toothpick in their piece of cake (they hold the layers together). Gloria said, "That means you're supposed to kiss the cook."

Well, Mark and Paul were at the age of having a distinct aversion to girl germs. So we (probably Gloria and I) decided it made more sense to kiss the person whose birthday it was. Prior to each birthday celebration, Gloria and I would be in the kitchen gleefully loading the cake with toothpicks. When it was Mark or Paul's birthday, I usually had to sneak up on them in order to be "allowed" to plant that big wet kiss on their cheek. And when it was my birthday, Mark and Paul would giggle and carry on trying to work up the courage to kiss a *girl*.

We all got older. The kisses became routine. And then one day it was Greg's birthday. Unknown to us all, Dad had loaded up one hand with frosting. Then he announced he had a toothpick and went over to give the birthday boy a kiss. While he kissed Greg on one cheek, he smeared the other cheek with frosting. The kids loved it. From that point forward the birthday person had to beware, as at any given moment someone may be lurking behind you with a handful of frosting.

I think it was after Grandma Johnson's birthday that we abolished the birthday smear. Although she tried to be a good sport about it, it was pretty clear she didn't share the same sense of glee the rest of us did."

7. Greg, after getting smeared with birthday frosting. Karen is watching for his reaction.

In the early days of Wok cooking I bought a Chinese cookbook with lots of how-tos and recipes for wok cookery. One interesting note is that I was warned in the book to start with an orderly kitchen. I soon learned how right they were. Utter chaos can ensue if the breakfast dishes aren't done before you start cooking in Chinese. The book is long gone, but I still remember that good advice.

Another wise piece of advice is to *always* have everything chopped, measured, and ready in little dishes before you start cooking. The cooks on TV always do that and I've discovered that it works for any sort of cooking. I remember being frantic many times because I had to chop something that I forgot and something else was burning while I was chopping. Now, I cut up vegetables and get things ready for cooking hours (and even a day) in advance. It really saves on sanity.

My first attempt with Chinese cooking was beef with celery. My own recipe evolved through the years, but the warning in that early cookbook was that once you serve this dish successfully, you may never move on through the book because this dish is so good. They were right.

Recipe: (Entrees) Beef with Celery

Turning 30

Time moved quickly and before I knew it, I turned 30 years old. Of course, Gene was out of town, and I suddenly realized that this was the height of my life. My dreams of being a professional singer were dashed, and I couldn't imagine ever going back to college. All I could see was cooking and laundry and taking care of a 15-room house and six children with a husband gone 5 days a week. I cried for three days.

After the pouting, I decided that I needed to do something to fulfill myself or I'd go crazy. So, besides singing in the church choir, I joined a local community theater. I got on the board of directors and then auditioned for a play. I paid Renee for babysitting and off I went several nights a week to rehearsals after getting everyone fed and settled for the evening. What fun! After a few weeks, I learned that I had the best of all worlds. I could sing and dance and act on stage, make important decisions as a member of the theater board, and work happily at home without the pressure of having an outside job. How great was that?!

8. Mother's Day, 1972. The awful-but-you-have-to-eat-it breakfast in bed. Mark, Paul, Lee, Gloria, and Karen.

Adopting the children

Gene and I wanted the children to feel like they really belonged together forever, and we talked about adoption for the five older ones. We brought up the subject and then let it go, wanting them to think about it. Sometime later, the older kids came to us when we were leaving on a trucking trip and asked what would happen to the little kids if something happened to us. It was time.

We started the process for Gene to adopt Paul, Mark and Karen, and for me to adopt Greg and Renee. This was a big step because their original birth certificates would be changed. We explained everything to all of the grandparents and to Jerry, who was of course Paul, Mark, and Karen's birth father. All agreed that it would be a better life for all of the children to be real brothers and sisters, even though Greg's birth certificate now lists me as his mother and my age at the time of his birth—10. An amusing fact for him to explain, for sure.

At this time my Dad was very ill with colon cancer and he worried about my children's future. As it happened, the adoption was final the day before he passed away. I called to be sure he knew that the children were really "Cannons," and he was very relieved to hear this news.

Ten-year old Mark, however, had different worries that we didn't know about. He had a friend who had lived in several foster homes and had actually been adopted once but returned because it didn't work out. This boy told Mark that being adopted meant that he would have to go live with another family.

When we were all washed and polished and lined up at court, the judge looked down his nose at the children and asked, "And what do all of you think about this?" Karen immediately piped up, "Mark doesn't want to get adopted." He slunk down in his chair and whispered, "I do, too." The judge went on with the formal procedure and the full story didn't come out until we were all seated for lunch at a restaurant afterwards. There were lots of tears and hugs and assurances that we would all continue to live together and Gene was now their "real Dad," a major relief to Mark, especially.

9. They're all real Cannons. Karen, Renee, Gloria, Greg, Mark, Paul, with Gene holding Lee. December 1972.

By the way, the restaurant was St. Cloud's Ace Bar and Café, famous for their baked snapping turtle. Here's my version.

Recipes (Entrees) Turtle, Oven Baked

Memorable trip

Cousin Phil was getting married in Iowa in the early 1970's. It was the perfect opportunity for all of us to have a wonderful vacation together, visit with the relatives in Iowa over the 4th of July and go on to see my mother in Nebraska. Total distance for the trip would be 1,200 miles or so; piece 'a cake!

We loaded our huge old (un-air-conditioned) station wagon with luggage, sandwiches and cookies, eight people and the dog, our poodle,

Nicky. No seatbelts were required in those days and safety car seats for kids were unheard of. Baby Lee sat in his little cloth and wire over-the-seat "car seat" between Gene and me in the front seat, or in his jumper chair in the "wayback," our term for the back end of the station wagon, along with several of the younger kids. With loud negotiations for window space already in progress and fighting over foot space in the wayback building, off we went in total oblivion.

Two hours into the trip we discovered that Paul suffered from carsickness. Luckily, the wayback was equipped with built-in bins alongside the walls. Cleaning them out wasn't easy, but Nicky helped.

By the time we hit Iowa, the lack of air conditioning was apparent. The potential of a week of 95+ degree temperatures didn't help our dispositions, but we settled in to the wind blowing through the car and we couldn't hear the yelling quite as much.

After nine hours or so we made it to the Wise Owl, the one old motel in the tiny town of Brayton, Iowa. The children exploded from the car, and jumped immediately into the proud motel's newly installed small, but wet, pool for which we gave mighty thanks to God.

With the wedding over, the punch drunk, and nylon stockings and ties removed, we all enjoyed watching the big 4th of July parade in Exira, a few miles away. We sat on blankets along the curb and watched with hundreds of farm families who came from miles around for this special annual event. We oohed and ahhed as a float or two went by, followed by strutting, baton twirling, majorettes leading the marching band. The band members, trapped and sweating in heavy wool uniforms, happily banged away on their drums and stepped higher as the majordomo raised his baton. There were clowns and horses and lots of candy thrown to eager grabbing young hands. The hot sun kept the flies away and we brushed off the ants that also liked the sticky sweet candies that lay melting in the street.

All of this was but foreplay for the focus of the parade. After much waiting and looking, here they came. The tractors. Dozens of them, in John Deere green and International Harvester red, freshly washed and shining so bright we had to look away when the sun played across the gleaming metal. There were tractors huge and small, with corn pickers, plows, balers and manure spreaders. There was farm machinery of every kind, lumbering slowly along the packed streets. Smoke rose into the air as the big machines belched, and the biting smells filled our senses. Our city-bred family was awed by the reverence on the faces of the watchers, and we could almost feel their dreams of owning such magnificence.

From Iowa, we ventured across Nebraska, and drove through endless cornfields. "Knee-high by the 4th of July," was the rule, in order for corn to mature properly, and every field was well over the mark, the kids proudly announced.

We made it to Diller with few mishaps, one being a flat tire on a lonely road. Of course we had to completely unload the wayback to get to the jack and the spare tire. With our belongings spread out over the highway, the kids all scampered into the weeds to play while Gene changed the tire and I fretted. With the tire repaired and the car reloaded, we started out. A blood curdling scream made it known that somebody found a wood-tick on their leg, thanks to the weed-walking. We stopped for extensive wood-tick inspection for all weed-walkers.

Leaving Mom's and heading home was close to unbearable with all of us tired and crabby, and temperatures hovering about 100 degrees. With so many of us plus the dog, we feared leaving somebody at our frequent stops, so our practice from the start of the trip was for everyone upon entering the car to call out "here," when I called their name. Sometimes Gene would remind me, "Honey, did you count the kids?" When all were accounted for we started out. Since we hadn't lost anybody yet, and this was the last leg of the trip, we began to get a little loose about getting everyone's "here," before driving off. Not good.

We stopped for gas in a small town and everyone took their turn in the restrooms, and Mark walked the dog. We all piled in the car, including the dog, and started down the road when I began the roll call. "Greg." "Here." "Renee." "Here." "Paul." "Here." "Mark." No answer. "Mark, quit goofing off." More silence. From somewhere in the back, "Hey Mom, Mark's not here!"

By this time we were several miles down the road. Gene quietly stopped, turned the car around, and headed back to the gas station. There was Mark, dejectedly sitting on the curb by the road with his head hanging. No tears yet, but they were close. We had a happy reunion and headed off toward home.

In all of our years together this was the one and only trip we took with all eight of us in one vehicle. Once was enough.

The perfect house

The house we lived in when Gene and I married was called the Dearing House, named after former owners. It was a landmark in St. Cloud, very near Tech high school, and not far from downtown. It was old and huge with two stairways to the second floor, a big one in front and a small one for the "servants." There were five bedrooms on the second floor, plus a finished attic, or loft, and an apartment in the basement. Gene and his first wife, Dee had bought it from a college art teacher who did some creative painting throughout, so it was in pretty bad shape. Gene and Dee did quite a bit of painting and fixing up, and after I moved in, we did more of the same.

It was great for entertaining and close to school for the kids, but for some reason, that house never really felt like my home. I felt like a guest and was never comfortable no matter how much I did to decorate it. After we had to call police because of a situation with one of the children and a man in the neighborhood, we decided to move.

Lots of changes ensued. Greg moved out with buddies and continued with college, Renee moved in with a friend soon after her graduation. The rest of us moved across town to what we called "the Centennial house," located in a development near the old St. Cloud airport. It was perfect.

Perfectly boring, we soon discovered. Our house was on a curvy street and all the houses looked alike. If Gene stayed too long at the Elks Club, he couldn't find the house. The boys couldn't bounce the basketball in the driveway because the neighbor lady yelled at them. We got a notice that we had to pay our share of the neighborhood dandelion poisoning. The lady across the street took out her garbage in her "old" mink.

The house may have been perfect, but we were not.

Gene's business travels were more frequent and he was seldom home.

We had a number of medical issues that I had to deal with alone, including Lee getting his arm caught in a conveyor belt at the grocery store. Our beautiful curious three and a half year-old boy spent weeks in the hospital having skin grafting. What a scary and terrible thing for him to endure and for me as well, because of the guilt I felt for what I saw as negligence in letting this happen.

What none of us knew as life unfolded, was that this painful experience would eventually result in Lee being able to go to college, when very likely there would have been no hope for that to happen.

An even worse medical predicament was suffered by Karen. She developed rheumatoid arthritis and had many episodes that caused her to be hospitalized and unable to walk for what turned out to be at least a couple of weeks a year all through her youth.

This horribly painful condition, also called RA, started when she was only five years old. She began to scoot around the house on her bottom, saying that her legs hurt. After many hot baths and Mom-type soothing, it didn't get better. RA was later confirmed by a biopsy of her knee.

Doctors put her on a massive program of aspirin in hopes to keep her joints from crippling, and she was not allowed to jump or run or participate in school gym activities. It was all that could be done at that time because little was known about RA.

At age 18, Karen was re-evaluated and taken off the aspirin. One morning soon after that she came down the stairs and said to me, "Mom, I just woke up."

I joked that it was about time, and she said, "No Mom, I feel like I just woke up after years of being asleep." Karen had been taking up to 25 adult aspirin a day for more than 13 years. It's a wonder that her stomach and digestive system survived.

We had hoped that she would out-grow the disease, as doctors had indicated early on, but we know that she will have joint pain all her life. There are other medications for it now, and they also determined that the type of RA she has is non-crippling, which is a small blessing.

Only another mother can know the agonies suffered when your child is in pain and you can't take the pain away.

Chapter 4

The farm

In 1975, after only two years in the "perfect" house, we "bought the farm." Gene was traveling heavily for his work and was rarely home. I didn't realize how really unhappy all of us were in that house until one Saturday Gene and I were sitting at the Country Club after lunch and when I said it was time to go home, he said "I don't want to go home."

What he meant was that he didn't ever want to go home to that house and neighborhood. It was stifling to all of us in its perfection, and nobody really felt comfortable there.

I picked up a newspaper lying nearby, that was already folded open to a photo of a hobby farm and listed by a realtor friend of ours. I said, "This is what you'd really like, right?" There was discussion about too expensive, bad timing, can't do it, etc. I insisted that we drive by the place and take a look anyway. From the wistful look on his face, I knew that this was the answer.

In my usual "take care of it" mode, the next day when Gene left town I arranged to tour the farm with our friend, the realtor. To make a long story short, we moved in November, and Gene was thrilled.

Here is a story written in 1995, more than 10 years after we left there, about moving to the farm and how one ragged old porch made it home for me.

The Porch

We moved to the farm during a three day blizzard. Our leisurely scheduled move over a pleasant Thanksgiving weekend, was instead a fractured scenario like the frenzied frozen flakes whirling helter skelter around us. Nothing happened in sequence. We were here, the movers were there.

We couldn't get to the farm to clean and paint. The movers were stuck in the snow somewhere with half of our belongings on the truck. We and the other half of our belongings were stuck in our house in town on its fashionable street that was always the last to be plowed. Finally, the roads were cleared and the move plowed on.

I dragged my aching body down the hall, tripping over my moon boots and struggling with the last heavy load of boxes, knowing I was at least three inches shorter than when I started the day. And there it was. In the clamor and excitement of finding this rambling old farmstead with enough rooms in the house for all of us and space to spare, plus all those wonder-filled barns and granaries, I had overlooked this porch at the end of the hall leading to the bedrooms. During one of the remodelings and shifting of rooms over its 60 year lifetime, this sad and lonely, fading porch ended up at the wrong end of the house. It was like the rest of the house took the detour to the new highway, and this room bumped along on the old road, toward the inevitable dead end.

It was dismal and dirty, with peeling paint hanging in strips from the wooden ceiling. There were rusty screens with hunks of cotton half stuffed in jagged holes to keep the flies out, to no avail judging by the piles of crusty corpses on the ledges and the floor. The snow was piled in the corners and all across the front where it blew through the unresisting screens. It was not very deep, only about 10 feet, but it was about 20 feet wide and there was a crooked screen door to the front yard. It looked like it hadn't really shut tight for several years. Sad it was, but from its sadness I gained strength and from the moment I saw it, I knew this porch would be my special place. I could hardly wait to start making it mine.

Eagerly, we painted and papered and repaired and replaced what needed to be done in the rest of the sturdy old house. With our collective energies we transposed it into a lovely home. When the new carpet went into the kitchen, I rescued just enough of the old green stuff from the trash to cover the cold cement of my old porch; its transformation was begun. My husband replaced the old screens with 10 new storm windows and a fancy metal door. I scrubbed and painted everything sparkling white and found an antique looking light fixture to replace the single bulb that was hanging by a ragged wire. When I topped it all off with a crisp curtain valance of nature's greens, I could feel that room smile.

With a family of eight plus various friends, significant others and hangers on, we needed lots of places to eat, so we put an old picnic table with benches on the porch and it became our favorite place for light suppers. Meals were often followed by noisy games of Crazy 8, or Go-to-the-Dump, or even Poker, and lots of Scrabble. My poor constipated vacuum cleaner choked on many a stray Scrabble letter hiding, or hidden, under the table.

I got a porch swing for Mother's Day, the wooden kind that seats two and hangs from the ceiling. I loved to sit sideways in the swing with my feet up and read on a lazy afternoon, or just daydream a little. Every time I sat there I looked up and smiled to myself when I saw the four little extra holes in the slatted wooden ceiling where Gene tried to find the stud to hang the swing. He was in a hurry to surprise me. There were only two holes then. Until the first time we both sat in the swing and one side came down with a whump. There were two more holes by the time he really found the stud. I'm sure if I mentioned them he'd have filled them in, but he forgot the holes and I felt good having them there. They sort of fit the room.

I dug up a scrawny looking bush from the ditch by the road and planted it outside the front windows. It turned out to be a wild rose and it flourished like a weed, producing a mass of delicate pink flowers every spring thereafter. Competing with the wild roses were the lilacs. Thousands and thousands of sweet purple-smelling lilacs bursting into bloom from century-old plantings grown wide with age. With the porch windows open and a breeze blowing, the smell was almost overpowering. The scent of those blossoms, especially in the morning as the sun dried up the dew, flavored my coffee with a perfume I could taste. Morning was my favorite time on the porch. As soon as the crowd was fed and launched, I fled with my coffee and newspaper to the quiet comfort of my porch. With Nicky, my elegant poodle-turned-farm-dog, curled at my feet, we both gathered strength for the tasks of the day. Nicky whimpered in her sleep, no doubt dreaming of chasing gophers or chickens. I wrote long newsy letters to the Grandmas, made lists of things to pick up in town later, or just watched the cedar trees standing at attention. There were exactly 55 cedar trees, tall and straight and planted in stately rows in the front yard. From my spot in the porch they looked like the trumpet section of a marching band, with arms upraised and ready to blow. Some trailing branches would cast moving shadows as the sun poked through and it looked like fringe from their uniforms waving gently.

Life goes on. The kids grew up, we moved on. Someone else is watching the sunrise from my porch now as I gobble a quick bite in our sleek apartment and dash off to shuffle papers in the work world. But the memories will always be mine, and can be gently awakened at the scent of wild roses, or lilacs, or cedar trees, or most anything at all.

Life on the farm

Greg and Renee were on their own by the time we moved to the farm, so we had only the four young ones with us. Mark was the resistant one and feared leaving his known school and neighborhood. He complained and whined mightily, but we knew that this would be good for everyone and with great difficulty dragged him along. After only a few days at the farm the kids and I went back to the old neighborhood for coffee with friends. When we got there, Mark said, "Boy, I'm glad we don't live here anymore—there wouldn't be anything to do!"

Thus began life on the farm. There were animals; a few laying hens were left by the previous owners, and of course we acquired many others including goats, a horse or two, chickens, ducks, even wild turkeys. There were fancy tumbling pigeons that lived in the barn and entertained us regularly with their beautiful soaring high in the sky, and then tumbling over and over until they almost hit the ground. We could have separated these birds and bred them for color and tumbling artistry, but nobody was ever interested enough to do it. We enjoyed the pigeons and they stayed around through all of our years there.

One time, when we were overloaded with young pigeons, I decided to cook some squab. Paul and Mark helped me gather a small bunch of young pigeons that were adult size and feathered out, just ready to leave the nest. We dressed them and I served a delicious dinner of roasted squab. They were moist and delicious, but only one time did we have an abundance of young birds to use them for a meal.

Recipe: (Entrees) Squab, Roasted

This might be the point to talk about eating our home-grown animals. Never really having grown up on a farm, I was a little squeamish about eating some kinds of meat or animals, and so was the rest of the family. The only things we could really eat without feeling bad were the birds, like chickens, ducks, geese and the like. These animals are not in the "cute and friendly" category, like Lee's lop-eared rabbits. The chickens were so nasty that we were eventually able to eat chicken on butchering day! We didn't raise any beef or pork and never butchered anything else.

When we moved to the farm Lee was about four years old. The hens that were left by the previous owners continued to lay eggs, and Lee loved to gather the warm eggs each morning. He would steal quietly in the door of the chicken house and feel gently in each nest for that special gift of the perfect egg. They were brown, or tan, or creamy white, and after we had taught him how to collect them, he loved to surprise me with his new-found treasures. He would go quietly on his own to the chicken house while I watched his progress from the kitchen window, and bring the eggs two at a time, held gently but securely in his hands. He proudly beamed while I praised him for being so careful, and then would tell a new story every morning about which chicken was looking sideways at him, the special noises they made as they talked with each other, or some other adventure that happened on the way to and from the chicken house.

One morning the phone rang just as Lee was leaving for the chicken house. While I chatted with a friend, I lost track of time and didn't realize that Lee had been gone for too long. Suddenly, he appeared at the door, tears smeared all over his dirty face, and telltale yellow and chicken-poo covered his shirt. Between his sobs and my guilty self-chastisement, it came out that when he got into the chicken house, the wind blew the door shut and the little piece of wood that locked it was turned. He was trapped! He finally got out by crawling out the little door near the floor where the chickens went in and out. He wasn't crying out of hurt or fear; he was crying because he broke the egg. He had put it in his shirt pocket while he crawled face-first out the door and down the ramp for the chickens, and the egg was smashed against his chest as he crawled. What a lesson—for both of us!

Here is a beautiful poem that Renee wrote for me about our family meals on the farm. Even though she never lived there, it was an important part of her life along with the rest of us.

THE FAMILY TABLE

By Renee (Sometime in the 70's on the Farm)

For the hours you spend planning family meals,
Forgotten Jello, chopped onions and potato peels —
The table that's set, eventually, with care,
And the scent of burning buns as we each take our chair . . .

We know in our hearts that the food is secondary,
It's each other's company that makes us merry.
As eyes meet eyes across your table,
And the conversation turns to a retold fable.

A place to make memories, then to keep them alive,
Some searching, some sharing, some rapping, some jive –
Over a table literally filled with food,
To see it gone in seconds, seems ever so rude.

But, as we push back our chairs and slowly disperse,
We share feelings that could never be put to verse –
Cause we've gotten to know each other one more time,
With the help of your rosemary, basil and thyme.

A place to gather, to laugh and to greet,
To pass the potatoes, the veggies, the meat –
What we're really passing is something quite rare,
It's the loving, the caring that each of us share.

So don't ever think that we don't see,
What our family table has turned out to be –
Or that your loving preparation has been a waste,
'Cause it's life, not food, you've given us to taste.

**10. A family dinner at the farm in the early 1980's:
Jason, Renee, Karen, Lee, Gene, Cassie, Bucky, Paul, Gloria**

I liked to try new recipes and would pour for hours through cookbooks at the kitchen table or in the front porch. I'd look carefully for something special to make for supper. Many days I'd get so engrossed in reading the cookbooks that I'd use up all my time and have to rush to make something quick for everyone to eat. So much for the gourmet meals I wanted to make.

I clipped recipes from the newspaper. One that sounded really nutritious and that I thought the kids would like was mashed carrots. It was simply carrots, boiled, drained and mashed, with some crushed parsley added for color. I made this delicious new treat for a time when Renee and her family were with us for dinner, including her adorable new baby, Jason. Unfortunately, the bright green specks of parsley added to the mushy orange carrots made it too familiar to Renee. She immediately informed everyone that my special vegetable looked like baby poop, and nobody would eat a bite.

Some years later I found another recipe for mashed carrots, but I leave out the parsley and this one is delicious.

Recipe: (Vegetables) Hutspot—Dutch Potatoes and Carrots

Soon after we moved to the farm, our friends, Patty and Lou Thach, decided that we needed a goat. Why, we'll never know, or where they got it. They presented us with a beautiful little goat, a chocolate brown, bouncing baby Toggenburg. The whole family was thrilled (okay, I had some reservations . . .) and we named her Plaches, after the Thaches. Of course, Plaches needed a fence, so the chicken yard became bigger, but there was plenty of room in the chicken house for little Plaches to be comfortable. Unfortunately, Plaches was smart. She soon learned to open the gate and feasted on any blooming flowers nearby, and the vegetable garden, to my distress.

After some prodding, Gene got a new latch for the gate, and along with a bagful of nuts and bolts, he set off for the barnyard to Plach-proof the gate. Plaches thought this was a new game and several times as Gene bent over to work, she ran between his legs. The kids and I watched from the house, and laughter was brewing. Soon, Plaches bumped him a little harder and over Gene went to the ground. He dropped the bag of nuts and bolts, and since paper is a favorite snack for goats, Plaches promptly ate it. The hardware fell to the ground, scattering in the grass, and Gene crawled around yelling at the goat and the world in general. You can imagine our delight in watching the whole episode.

Somehow, Plaches survived this event and grew fat and happy in her new home, and soon we acquired another gentle female, named Princess. The children wanted little ones, so we began looking for options. In our negotiations for a papa goat, we learned that stud fees would be $50, but the owner was persistent and ended with, "If you buy him you can have him for $5, and I'll deliver." Did we see through this ruse? Ha! A handsome Billy goat soon appeared, and was immediately dubbed King Arthur.

Paul and Mark "did the chores" each day for all of the animals, and hauled water and feed to the various creatures. They were always careful with King Arthur, and learned quickly that his silly "dancing" was actually a prelude to an aggressive attack, and his horns were sharp and dangerous. The tree in the chicken yard was quickly climbed on several occasions when King Arthur took after the boys.

Another distinctive feature about male goats is that they pee on themselves to smell good for the "girls." In winter this results in yellow icicles hanging from their fur. Attractive to their kind, perhaps, but this became the last straw.

King Arthur didn't live with us long. I'm embarrassed to say that we passed him off in pretty much the same way we got him, to some unsuspecting people who, like us, didn't understand that male goats are very much different than gentle females. The new family happily drove away with King Arthur's yellow icicles already beginning to melt in their clean pickup truck.

Meanwhile, King Arthur did his job, and we had all the babies we wanted. We also had all the goat milk we wanted, and more. To get it, Gene and Mark built a goat milking stand. It was surely a one-of-a-kind affair that had a tray for treats, a ramp for the goat to walk up, and a clamp for her head. The milker sat on a straw bale and milked away in comfort while the goat munched on goat chow.

The milk, while very nutritious and rich, was too different from the ordinary skim milk we usually drank, so instead, I cooked with it. We had goat milk puddings, casseroles, and soups. I even made goat milk ice cream and it was great. It also made terrific macaroni and cheese.

Recipe: (Entrees) Macaroni and Cheese

We raised several kinds of ducks, including Mallards, for which you need a permit because they are considered wild, and Muscovys. The Mallard ducks were small and beautiful, very smart, and tasted pretty good. We didn't like to eat them because they were so pretty, and I think we only raised one batch of Mallards. They had beautifully colored feathers that were iridescent and they strutted around the barnyard obeying nature's laws, but never ours. The Muscovys, on the other hand, were big white ugly ducks with not much smarts. We didn't mind eating them because they were just too dumb to survive the winter, and they really were delicious.

For example, when the boys would fill their water dishes on winter mornings, some of the big guys would stand in the water because it felt warm on their feet. Unfortunately, they didn't get out in time and their feet froze, trapping them in the water pans. Paul and Mark took pity on them and many times after school they would sneak a frozen footed duck into the basement shower to thaw out.

Unfortunately, the ducks didn't stay in the shower once their feet felt better, and they'd have the whole room pretty much carpeted in duck poop before the boys remembered they were there.

This was the case on a special weekend when Renee's baby Jason was baptized. We had a celebration at our house after the baptism with the other set of grandparents and other relatives there for the party. While I was busy in the kitchen getting dinner ready, and dozens of people filled the house, Grandpa Denne went looking downstairs for a bathroom. He quietly came up the stairs with a shocked look on his face, and said, "Did you know there's a duck in your bathroom?" Needless to say, the boys learned quickly how to wash a bathroom floor.

Recipe (Entrees) Duck Casserole

The following story, while satirical, of course, is actually true. I did bring home almost 100 little roosters and I had no clue how to deal with them or any other animal at that time. It was written about 1976, so the costs involved would be much higher today. Gene's mother Daisy Cannon, was a "chicken expert," having raised many throughout her life. She was trying to be kind when I excitedly told her what I had done. She said, "Well, I wish you well, but I can't think of a single good thing about a Leghorn rooster." I did get smarter, however, and the next year and those following, I ordered 100 fryer chickens—not Leghorns and not roosters of any kind.

With Free You Get Jack the Ripper

"Twenty-five FREE chicks with 50 pound feed purchase." The sign in the feed store window reeled me in after securely setting its hook with my second glance at the bait, that word, "FREE." What a deal! How could I say no? After all, we had just moved to the country for that precise purpose—to save money by living off the land, growing our own vegetables, raising a few animals. I could hardly wait.

The ride home was slow, but exciting, what with 100 loudly peeping, fuzzy, little, yellow chicks (after all, if 25 are good, 100 must be better!) and the trunk filled with several 100 pound bags of feed (only $14 each). Visions of giant fryer thighs pecked at my brain.

The first few days were really fun. I kept the baby chicks in a playpen (only $15 at a garage sale) in the granary, using some cute little things that you put on a fruit jar (only $3 each) for their water, and several special tiny metal feeders (only $10 each) for their grain. I only had to check them about every 30 minutes or so for that first week. I learned early on that young chickens tend to peck each other and some didn't give up until the other guy was dead. We managed to only lose about 10 or so before I put up some red bandannas ($1 each) for them to attack instead.

Their sweet yellow fuzz soon was replaced by scraggly feathers and they had a sort of patchwork look about them. One in particular that we called

Daddy Long Legs, looked like he got in a losing battle with the leaf mulcher. Long Legs never did lose that mangled look.

When we got the chicken house repaired (only $200 for a new roof, one window and a door) and the fence put up ($150) we moved the chicks to their new home. They loved their new galvanized metal feeders ($19.95 each) and gobbled up feed like crazy. Of course the feed store knew just what kind of waterers we needed as the chickens grew ($45.00 for 3). They were also glad to help us with the right vitamins and high protein feed ($16.00 a bag) after some of the chicks developed crooked legs and died because we thought they could just eat plain oats and corn.

We learned that our chicks were Leghorns. Leghorns are highly rated for being wonderful laying hens, though we never did find out much that roosters were good for. It's not easy for the average person to tell the difference between the genders of chickens when they're small. We had to wait until they were old enough to start crowing. Imagine our fun when we were joyfully awakened about 4:30 one morning by the adolescent croaking/crowing of 75 young Leghorn roosters. What a thrill!

Watching them through the summer as they grew was very educational. Young roosters are quite competitive and they just love to peck at things with their sharp little beaks. They really loved it when I would come into the chicken yard five or six times a day with feed or water or fresh straw ($2 per bale). They would come rushing at me pecking away at my knee-high, steel-toed boots ($59.95) and sometimes even reach above to my insulated heavy twill coveralls ($65), so eager they were to see me. Because of his unique personality and behaviors, we renamed Long Legs. He appropriately became "Jack the Ripper."

When full grown the roosters were about two and a half feet tall and weighed two pounds, as opposed to the plumper, slower moving hens at about six pounds. Though we would have preferred a more balanced ratio, we were happy with our five young hens. Unfortunately, nature being what it is, we humans aren't the only ones who like the taste of chicken. There was an adorable raccoon family living in the nearby woods, and they were hungry, too. We provided them with several tasty midnight meals.

One fat hen survived long enough to become our Thanksgiving dinner, and delicious she was! Quite a few of the roosters made it to the table, though it did take two of them to make a meal for our family of six. I must say that Jack made a particularly satisfying stew.

The costs involved in raising these wonderful, feathered, culinary delights amounted to about $5.65 per pound. Of course this did not consider the time spent in caring for them as this surely was measured in entertainment. All in all, our experience in raising chickens was actually one of the most financially profitable encountered during our years on the farm, living off the land, growing our own vegetables, and raising a few animals.

Chicken Butchering

Chicken butchering was quite an exciting event. My Mother came one year and she was amazing. She could clean a chicken faster than you could say "feather." We rented an electric chicken plucker that year and Mom was in charge of it. It was a machine with rubber "fingers" that whirled around and slapped the feathers off when you held the chicken just right. Mom was in her late 80s then and six of us could barely keep up with her. Somebody said later that there were chicken feathers blown to seven counties that day.

At the beginning, it took at least a couple of days to take care of all the chickens, but toward the end of our farm years, we could butcher 100 in a day, and even eat chicken for dinner the very night of butchering.

11. Grandma Jan Grone mastering the electric chicken plucker, 1983.

Everybody had a job. Paul and Mark caught chickens with the bent wire thing that they used to snag a foot. Gene chopped heads and stuffed them to bleed in the unique cone-shaped stainless steel piece that was nailed to a tree. That way they didn't flop around and get bruised. I dunked them in boiling water in the canner kept hot on the grill, and peeled off the first feathers. Mom or some other poor soul took off the rest of the feathers by hand or with the chicken plucker. Karen and whomever else we persuaded each year to help us, gutted them and helped Gene clean them out. I gave them the final look-over and wash, and put them in bags ready for the freezer. Whew!

At the beginning it was harder. We all felt bad about killing the animals and it was all so nasty—yuk! But at the end, we were so relieved to be done with those horrible, pecking, unfeeling creatures, that eating them was a delight! We always shared the end result with whoever helped us, Bucky and his wife Cassie many times, and others. Many of the chickens weighed 5-6 pounds dressed, and they were delicious.

Recipes: Chicken: roasted, fried, stewed, soup and more

Good Times

The farm years were a wealth of good times. Much work, yes, but it seemed to be fun work. Gene was able to cut down on his business travel and loved to come home to his '49 Ford tractor. He would hitch up a trailer to the tractor, fill a barrel with water and drive around the perimeter of the property to water trees. Our yellow lab, Honey, would ride on the trailer as well. Gene got a blade for the tractor and the driveway got graded a lot whether it needed it or not. When we left the farm, I think that was the hardest part for him, to leave his tractor.

Here's a little piece about an early winter morning and the tractor.

Memorable Morning

Early morning with light snow on the ground. Gene goes out for his car, sees tractor tracks leaving the barn and heading out through neighbor's yard. Comes in, wakes Gloria, "Did you let somebody use my tractor?" No way—antique 1949 Ford tractor is Gene's pride and joy. It gets better treatment than Gloria. They look at each other. No words needed. Gene goes upstairs, grabs Mark, says, "Where's my tractor?"

"Gee Dad, it's like this—we were at the gravel pit with the pickup and it got stuck."

"What gravel pit? How did the pickup get stuck?"

"Well, we were trying to see how far up the gravel mountain we could go before the truck got stuck, and it got stuck. We really buried that puppy. So we came home and got the tractor to pull out the pickup. We didn't want to wake you or anything, seeing as how you need your sleep and all, so we drove out through the neighbor's yard. It was cold, too. Man, the gravel pit is at least 10 miles away and that tractor doesn't go very fast. Well we got to the gravel pit and it just died."

"It just died. Do you mean to tell me that both my pickup and my tractor are 10 miles away at somebody's private property gravel pit and it just died?!!"

"Yeah, Dad. I was gonna tell you later."

Rest of story is X rated.

12. A snowy day for Paul and Gene and the precious '49 Ford N, about 1978.

All of the kids learned to work when we lived on the farm and they did it willingly because there was plenty of time to play, too. Paul was a good worker when we all worked together, but we would have to watch him as he would wander off and not come back. When we went looking, we'd invariably find him bent over reading something. An open magazine, a food box, a tiny piece of newspaper, anything with words printed on it drew him like a magnet. He wouldn't even sit down, just bend over and read whatever it was that caught his eye.

All of the children did animal chores and helped in the big garden. There was a rule in the summer that each had to weed a row before they could go off for the day with friends, and my firmness was known. One time Mark's friend called and asked, "Hey Mark, can you go swimming today or does your Mom have you chained to a tomato plant?"

Friendships

Most of our friendships in those days revolved around the Elks Club. Gene had been a member for years and spent a lot of time there—sometimes too much for my liking. I went to parties and activities and was asked to sing there for a dinner function. I asked a friend to do something with me and wrote a short program that went over well. The next year I was asked again, so I invited more people to be involved. That was the beginning of what came to be called the Elks Variety Show. For 10 years, my talented friends Shirley and Carlotta and I wrote the scripts, most of the jokes and many ridiculous songs. The three of us produced the show, and I directed it. Shirley and Carlotta played the piano, and we all sang and danced and did silly comedy along with a cast that grew to more than 40 people.

It was sort of like the old "Laugh In" show where people did short one-liners in between "good" singing and dancing acts. We had a band that played with us and for most of those years we did an annual two night sold-out dinner show for audiences of more than 150 people. What a run! It was a great time, great friendships and fun people.

13. A small group of the Elks Variety Show cast, around 1981. I'm at top left, and Gene is at bottom left.

Many of our gatherings, whether for rehearsals or just for a party, were potluck. I was always told to bring brownies and lemon bars.

Recipe: (Desserts) Brownies and lemon bars

Lots of Music

During those years I took care of my friend Mary's children after school. When it came time for them to have piano lessons, Mary asked me to teach them as I was already giving some voice lessons to adults. When I said that I didn't know how to teach piano, she said, glibly, "Well take a class." So I did. With very little college except for some rudimentary music classes, I went to St. Cloud State University and took a graduate course in piano pedagogy. I got the highest grade in the class, and was told that the piece I wrote for the final was used for a long time afterwards as an example of how to write a teaching piece. I'm not bragging here, I'm just amazed!

Anyway, I taught beginner piano to Dana and Susan plus a whole bunch of other neighbor kids for several years. I wasn't a great teacher as I've never been a good pianist myself. Any student who really showed promise I sent on to other better teachers, but it was thrilling to watch children learn to love music under my watch.

The piano kids got off the bus at our house for lessons and were always hungry when they arrived. I had treats ready for them and my own kids before we did lessons.

Recipes: (Desserts) Chocolate Chip Oatmeal Bars, Toffee Bars, Angel Cookies

Music was a big part of all of our lives while we lived on the farm, particularly. The kids all played some sort of instrument or sang in school choirs. Karen and Lee were in 4-H and I led their Share-the-Fun skits, usually doing a musical number of some sort.

From the time we moved to St. Cloud we went to Bethlehem Lutheran Church, and I sang in the choir all the time we lived there. Most of that time I also sang with the Ladies Ensemble. This was a group of seven women who sang for church services and special events and entertained at many nursing homes. We grew close through the years and our music ministry was very meaningful to all of us. One of my best memories is singing each year at the St. Cloud Veteran's Hospital right before Christmas. This was a touching way for me to feel the real meaning of Christmas, and I know we boosted the spirits of many patients there.

I did singing telegrams, crazy as it sounds. I was going to start up that business myself, but a friend beat me to it and asked if I would do some "gigs" to help him get going. I wrote a silly song for each one after getting information about the party receiving the "Music Gram" as it was called. I wore a cute music sweater and hat, went to bowling alleys, offices, homes, restaurants, and more. I'd blow my whistle to get attention, then sing the song at peak volume, delightfully embarrassing whoever I was singing to. It was a lot of fun for me and for the people I honored, and I did this for a good five years; way more than a "few gigs."

The Cannon Reunions

The Cannon family reunions are held every two years in the tiny town of Brayton, Iowa.

When Gene's mother, Daisy, passed away at age 97 in July 1984, the family agreed to continue to get together every two years around the 4th of July. The reunions are still going strong and the next generation is taking over. It was again my family's responsibility to plan the event in 2008. Unfortunately, only Renee's family made it to Iowa because the others had work or financial problems and couldn't make it. Onno and I were there, too, and we did the whole scene; wrapped our arms around the tree in the middle of the road (or tried to) oohed over the plow in the oak tree (almost hidden now) toured the cemeteries, and had our pictures taken with Albert the Bull, from his best side, of course.

In 1994, our family was in charge of the reunion, and we made 25 pounds of Gene's Hash to serve everyone who came from the East Coast, West Coast, and many places in between. Here is his tongue-in-cheek recipe.

Recipe: (Entrees) Hash

The American Trucking Associations' annual convention was something that I looked forward to as a chance for Gene and me to get away. He had to work the conventions, of course, and I attended most meetings and sessions, too. Sometimes we had someone come to the house to watch the children while we were gone, and a couple of times Renee stayed with them. Once Gene and I drove to Washington DC for the convention, and when it was over, Karen and Lee flew out to join us. We used the subway system to pick them up from the airport, and when we got out of the train in the huge dome at Union Station, Lee was overwhelmed by the enormity of it all. He whispered, "Man, this is just like Star Wars!"

We drove up the East Coast to visit Gene's brother Don and his family of five beautiful daughters. We had a wonderful time and Don's wife Marion fixed a huge lobster. It was the first time I ever saw a lobster being stuffed—alive—into a big steaming copper pot. It was delicious. There was so much meat on this enormous lobster of almost seven pounds that we all ate our fill and Marion made lobster salad the next day.

Don and Marion had come to see us at the farm a few years before, and all of the kids had a grand time together. They came in an old painted up school bus that Don had fixed up. Lee called it "The Bucket," and the name stuck for all the time they had the bus.

A Treasure Found

Recently, I came across a torn page out of a notebook from 1982. In one of my sporadic efforts at keeping a record of activities or at least some of the events that I sang for, I made these scratchings from mid-January to April 4, 1982 (it makes me tired to read it now!):

Dear Book,

It looks like this is as close to a diary as I'm going to get—the problem is I keep forgetting all the things I sing for and do, and it creates problems later, like I can't remember what I sang for a political event or a trucking banquet or the like, and now I've been asked back for the next occasion. So, here goes:

January 1982: ATS Drivers dinner; did a part of the variety show. I sang "Hello Again," and did a duet with Gene of "Marshmallow World." Sang with chorus for a '50s medley and "Hallelujah."

- 1-18-82: gave blood, started guitar lessons for 6 weeks (didn't learn anything!)
- Early February: Karen in hospital for 2 weeks with arthritis.
- 2-18-82: BLCW (Bethlehem Lutheran Church Women)—sang duet with Sylvia G. "This Song's for You," Nova played.
- 2-20-82: ATS Safety dinner, sang "Let There Be Peace on Earth." Sharon K. played.
- 2-25-82: went to lecture at State (St. Cloud State University) by Peg Meier, author of "Bring Warm Clothes." Nice. Bought the book.
- 2-28-82: did liturgy for 9:30 service. Went to Karen's capping ceremony at St. Cloud Hospital for Jr. Volunteers.
- 3-1-82: State Driver of the Year award banquet, Prom Center, St. Paul. Sang "Let There Be Peace on Earth." Sharon K. played and Gene

- spoke on safety. This was the 4th year that I've sung for this event. I hope they don't ask me again, getting boring for audience. (*note: I sang for this event for the next 9 years.*)
- 3-18 to 2-1-82: went to Florida with friends Bob and Gloria, good time!
- 3-24-82: Sang for Lenten service "What a Friend We Have in Jesus," with Ladies Ensemble. Rehearsed with Leatrice (flute) for solo on Sunday.
- 3-25-82: Ensemble practice in am, Elks show rehearsal 7:00 pm
- 3-26-82: Sauk Rapids, big Share the Fun night with Foley acts also, 13 in all, Wide Horizons came in 3rd. I helped get acts on stage and off and just oversaw all backstage stuff; got judges oriented and helped them add scores. Lot of work!
- 3-27-82: Sherburne County political convention all day in Big Lake. Both Gene and me delegates, but Gene tied up at work. Got home at 6, went to dinner at Elks at 7.
- 3-28-82: Sang 8 and 9:30 at church, liturgy and solo with Leatrice on flute; "This Song's for You," contemporary and pretty. At noon, judged Share the Fun skits and one-act plays for Stearns County in Albany, got paid $15 for it.
- 3-30-82: Sang with ensemble at St Cloud Manor nursing home.
- 4-4-82: Solo with choir for both services, "Ride on Jesus."

Life Lessons

The farm years were filled with goings-on of every kind. How lucky we were to have that beautiful place to spread and grow, to work and play, and to love each other. I'll be forever grateful for those years of being home when the kids came home from school. For being there when Paul ran screaming with excitement to tell me "Bessie (a goat) had a baby!" For being there to watch Lee "pick" eggs, still warm from the chickens; to see Karen plant flowers in the window box of her playhouse; to watch Paul and Mark and the neighbor boys build an ice fishing house in the driveway.

Oh yes, the fish house . . . built with expensive oak flooring that Gene had been hiding in the barn to use for some special project. The boys thought it was perfect for the fish house. Once built, the fish house was so heavy that it never got moved out of the driveway all winter. These four boys and their friends would light a fire in the little furnace and play cards out there by the hour for the whole winter. The neighbors would drive by and then call, asking, "Are you catching much in your driveway?"

Chapter 5

After the farm

In 1986, Gene was feeling unchallenged, out of control, and just plain out of it, with his work situation. He was unclear and wary about new directions with the company he worked for, and weary from years of too much traveling. His stress level was high, and he decided that his health was more important than his future with the company. I was shocked at his decision to leave the company and tried to help him work through his problems. I was not successful. Gene quit his job after 25 years of devoted commitment to many coworkers and friends, and to growing this company that he loved.

The owner of the firm was not at all happy with Gene's resignation. I believe that he might have felt betrayed by Gene's leaving, and their relationship that had weathered many storms through the years, soured. Whatever happened, happened, and nothing could change the outcome. Gene left the company, and with glum sadness as well as hopeful anticipation, we moved away from our hobby farm and all of the wonderful memories there.

Gene's new office was in South St. Paul where he started Cole Trucking along with backing from an old friend. It was a new idea in trucking at that time, hauling big but light-weight freight with smaller trucks. They bought some light-weight trailers and with a good customer-base, they hired drivers and started hauling.

All of the children but Lee were on their own by that time. Lee was 15 and doing his permit driving. We spent several weekends looking at where to live in the Twin City area, and to his delight, Lee did most of the driving. There were many beautiful Eastern suburbs close to South St. Paul, so we decided to let Lee choose where he wanted to go to school and we'd get a house in that area. He chose Stillwater High School, so we rented and eventually bought a modest house in the nearby small town of Lake Elmo and across the street from the lake after which the town is named.

Stillwater High School came to be an excellent choice for Lee and he was very successful there. He did well in school and played trombone in the band and a jazz band. He also joined the swim team and eventually was made co-captain. Gene and I cheered loudly along with the other parents at swim meets.

At the time we moved from St. Cloud, I was expecting to work at Cole Trucking also, in some office position. However, Gene was taking a small salary from the new young company to get it well started, and it became necessary for me to find an income from someplace else.

Away I went again into a new world. I hopefully submitted my old and thin resume at many companies, but didn't have much success. At this point I could type fast, but that was about my limit in office skills. Unfortunately, even though I had served on a board of directors and performed as secretary for several organizations, I had 16 years of unpaid experience as a Mom, which wasn't valued by employers. I had no education except for music, and no computer skills; a sad state of affairs.

I worked for a time with a temporary agency to get some experience, and that helped. I finally got hired as a receptionist for a company in a nearby town, and moved up the ladder pretty quickly there when they discovered that I was able to do more than they expected. However, I kept looking for a company and a job that I felt really good about. I was finally hired by EMA, Inc., an engineering firm in Roseville, Minnesota. They saw my potential and I was happy and motivated to work for a company that helped to provide clean water all over the country.

When the three of us got comfortable in Lake Elmo, we planned to take our time church-shopping and intended to look at several churches in the area before we joined one. However, the moment we walked in the door at Christ Lutheran Church in beautiful downtown Lake Elmo, we all felt at home and such a feeling of peace, that we saw no need to look further. I joined the choir and Gene ushered until he could no longer walk. Lee got involved in youth activities and we all worked for what was fondly called, "The Sauerkraut Supper." This is still an annual dinner of roast pork, sauerkraut, mashed rutabagas (no kidding!) mashed potatoes, gravy, and homemade pie. The church feeds more than a thousand people for this meal and everyone in the church works. In this heavily German community, meals like this are common, and it was a real switch from the Norwegian fare in St. Cloud. Here are some recipes that are typically German.

Recipe: Vegetable Hot Dish (Minnesota's name) or Vegetable Casserole (from any other part of the country)

Recipe: Roast Pork

Meanwhile, Gene kept struggling to build Cole Trucking. In spite of horrendous interest rates, cutthroat competition, and a generally poor business climate, he provided a good livelihood for many drivers and workers for several years in the lightweight voluminous freight business. He ordered specially built light-weight trailers and had at least a dozen company drivers or owner-operators and authority to haul all over the U.S.

Gene had tried for years to get his previous company to start this sort of business, but they were not interested. Once Gene got going, several other companies started their own similar services and competed directly with him. With the resources of much larger companies against him, Gene had a hard time keeping his new customers from being subtly stolen. To add to these difficulties, a trusted employee began to misuse funds, and the company spiraled down.

When the savings and loan fiasco happened in 1991, the examiners came and the bank that Gene worked with called in his loan. They demanded that he pay them $60,000 cash immediately or he would be out of business. Gene didn't have it.

Later, my understanding was that on the command of the examiners, 27 businesses went down that day. Yes, these were businesses on the edge. They were hoping against hope that "their ship would come in." Even so, I can't imagine the thoughts of the person or persons who basically pulled the rug out from under that many people. Did they get a sense of power? Or was it as hard as I would think it to be. To destroy the hopes and dreams of all of the owners and employees of 27 businesses in one day is more than hard to imagine, it's devastating.

That afternoon Gene called me at work and said that I'd better get over to South St. Paul right away. Representatives from the bank were hauling away the office furniture and were ready to lock the doors of Cole Trucking forever. When I got there, the office was already empty and Gene looked totally drained himself. We were both stunned at the suddenness of it all, but there was nothing we could do.

Sadly, Gene had put all of our savings and retirement money into the company, and had also taken a large second mortgage on our house. After some months of trying to save the house by making huge payments, we had to let it go. His company car was taken, the house was sold and all proceeds went to the bank. We lost everything that we had worked for and saved for our whole lives.

Recovering from a stunning event like this is difficult at best. I don't think that many people really knew how serious and devastating this was or what was actually happening to us at the time. We covered up a lot in order to spare ourselves the shock and pity in the eyes of others. And, I buried my feelings because of the terrible toll I knew this was taking on Gene. There are people who start and lose companies multiple times and they seem to personally come out on top. Not for Gene. This was humiliating beyond his acceptance and he was totally devastated.

These were hard times, but we were in it together and if anything, this blow brought us closer together. We put a bottle of champagne in the fridge for the new owners of our house, hugged our neighbors goodbye, and moved to an apartment in Maplewood, Minnesota, closer to my work.

Fortunately, I was doing well at EMA. We had wisely determined at the beginning that I should not work at Cole Trucking so that we could have income and benefits from elsewhere. Gene had been taking a small salary from the company in order to help the business succeed, so my outside income was crucial.

I did mid-level clerical support when I started with EMA. The company fortunately recognized my potential and supported further education, while promoting me to higher positions several times. My youngest son Lee and I started college at the same time in the fall of 1989. I was taking classes in evening and weekend courses, and earned an Associate's Degree about the time that Lee got his Bachelor's Degree. I continued studies at Metropolitan University, with 80 percent of costs paid by EMA.

Lee went to college at Eau Claire, Wisconsin, and the trust money from his childhood arm accident was safely there for him. Thankfully, the bankers were not able to touch those funds in the bankruptcy of the company.

Gene was suffering. We were forced to take personal and business bankruptcy, which was a huge blow to his sense of responsibility and integrity. He worked for others for several years after that and seemed to do well, but he never really recovered from the emotional trauma of failing, as he saw it. I believe that the cancer that eventually took his life started from the emotional trauma and shock of the business going down.

Gene had a variety of jobs for the next few years, and stayed active in many trucking associations. He was Secretary of the Stillwater Elks Lodge for many years, and he even worked for Bradshaw Funeral Services in Stillwater and liked it. When he was helping for a funeral one time, a little boy came to him and looked up, astonished, at the beautiful high dome of the church. The boy asked,

"Is this the Capital?" Gene answered, "Well it does sort of look like it, doesn't it." The boy asked again, "Are you the President?"

Gene finally worked as a guide at the Minnesota Science Museum in St. Paul, and said often that this was the best job he ever had. He loved watching the children get excited about the exhibits, and helping people there. Eventually, his prostate cancer, which was discovered very late in the game, metastasized to the bone, and even with several surgeries and hip replacements, the prognosis was not good.

We lived for five years in the apartment, and then were able to buy a two-level townhouse right around the corner, still in Maplewood, Minnesota. It was a comfortable place for us and we became acquainted with our delightful neighbor, Paula, who bonded with Gene immediately. Paula is a single woman, successful in business and she and Gene spent long hours discussing business issues and problems. Paula became one of the family in holiday gatherings, and always brings her wonderful fudge to share.

Recipe: Fudge (Paula's)

In 1995, I finally earned a Bachelor of Arts Degree in Communications from Metropolitan University in St. Paul. It was a long process, but one that I will be forever grateful for achieving. EMA promoted me to consulting status and I began yet another career.

In the years that I was doing communications consulting and traveling—yes, the shoe was on the other foot now—Gene was home more and liked to experiment in the kitchen. He found a recipe in the paper one day for a prize winning cake. The recipe was the grand-prize winner of a big baking contest and had been put together by a man. Well, not to be outdone, Gene decided that he could make a prize-winner too, and he made some variations to the recipe he found. It was delicious! Very rich and fattening, of course, but really good.

Disastrous consequences happened, however, when we invited our friends Joan and Ron over for dinner with the potential prize-winner cake for dessert. Joan had been having some problems and thought she might be allergic to certain things. Unknowingly, we had a pretty heavy dinner that evening, and topped it all off with the cake. Joan got violently ill on the way home and ended up in the hospital. What happened was that the richness of the food put her in an insulin reaction mode, and they discovered that night that she had undiagnosed diabetes. If you try this recipe, beware!

Recipe: Macadamia Nut Cake

Goodbye to Mom

Mom and Dad had retired to Nebraska in 1971, to be near Dad's sister's family (my beloved Uncle Joe and Aunt Florence) and because it was a very economical place to live. They bought a little house and immediately built a big garage and patio. Sadly, Dad passed away in December 1972 from complications of colon cancer and never got to really enjoy retirement.

Mom stayed in Nebraska and the next year married Irl Grone, a gentle older man who was very good to her. He was a retired rancher who sold his cattle farm and moved into her house. Mom made life fun for Irl and they had five good years together when Irl passed away. Irl's son Dean and his wife Marge, took wonderful care of Mom for the rest of her life, and I am forever grateful to them for this.

After Irl died I approached her about possibly moving back to Minnesota, and Mom said about Nebraska, "This is my home now, and I am happier here than anywhere I've ever lived."

She became a leader in the community by helping in the senior center and, in her 90's, driving the "old people" around town. The people loved to hear her do comic readings and she always had them laughing. Her sense of humor was terrific and when I called after she had cataract surgery at age 90, she said, "I have good news and bad news. The bad news is that I can see that I have wrinkles. The good news is that all my friends have wrinkles, too!"

Mom liked to play cards and for the last several years of her life she had a party every Friday night at her house, sometimes with 4 or 5 card tables full of noisy ladies having a great time. There was always dessert, sometimes a plain white cake with her special chocolate frosting or anything sweet.

Recipe: (Desserts) Chocolate Frosting
Queen Elizabeth II Cake
Rhubarb Cake
Brownies (1-2-3)

Through it all, she quilted, making dozens of beautiful and colorful quilts for family and friends. Many times I recognized an old dress or shirt in the quilting squares, cleverly hidden in intricate patterns. Mom recycled before we even knew the word!

In January 2002, Dean called with devastating news. We knew that Mom was not feeling well—stomach problems, she said. Dean said that when he took Mom to get checked, she was hospitalized and the doctors told him that she had cancer. He was afraid that if she found out that news, that she would not live long. I knew that he was right. Mom didn't like sick people and she hated being sick herself, which was rare. She was terrified of the word "cancer." Sure enough, the doctors, by law, had to tell her and she immediately seemed to "give in" to the disease and became extremely ill with fast-spreading melanoma.

I was very busy dealing with Gene's health at that time as he was having another surgery on his hip, so I wasn't able to go to Nebraska right then. Bucky was caught by work problems, so I spoke with my sister Fran and brother Neil to see if they could be with Mom until I could get there. I was so grateful that Neil went from Washington, DC even though he didn't think things were all that serious. He took care of Mom for a couple of weeks, and realized quickly that she wasn't going to come out of this at age 95. Fran also went to Nebraska from Hawaii, and Bucky and I got there with only days to spare. Mom died in her home with Bucky's wife Cassie and me holding her hand and I was singing from her hymnal. I was singing, "Prepare the Royal Highway," when a single tear rolled down her cheek and she gave her last sigh. It was March 23, 2002.

For Jan Grone's funeral, we collected many of the quilts she had hand-made, covering the backs of every pew in the church. It made a striking picture and created a festive atmosphere that was appropriate for the colorful and joyful life she led in Nebraska.

14. Janet Grone with some of the dozens of handmade quilts she made in her 30 years in Diller, Nebraska.

Cursillo

Gene and I were invited to attend a unique spiritual event that changed our lives forever. It was known as Cursillo, a Spanish term that means Renewal, or as the Lutheran version is known, Via de Cristo, the Way of the Cross. A group of our friends from Christ Lutheran Church had attended and Joan and Ron Johnson sponsored us for our weekend. Gene particularly, was truly moved by this experience and in a beautiful sermon that he gave in early 2002 at church, he said:

> My weekend led me to understand that each of us is given a "Holy Spirit," that is with us from birth to the end of our life on earth. God knocks on the door to our spirits, but it's up to us to open that door to let him into our heart and soul. Only then can we expect the miracle of everlasting life, when God transforms our faith to give us peace of mind, body, and spirit.
>
> When I left that Cursillo weekend in January 1999, I felt that Jesus had touched me and that God's presence was with me forever. My entire life changed. Living under the shadow of the cross means to me that I am covered and surrounded by His comforting presence, forever.
>
> Always remember that life is not measured by the number of breaths we take, but by the moments that take our breath away. Yesterday is history, tomorrow is a mystery. Today is a *gift*—that's why we call it the present.

We lived in the Maplewood townhouse five years. Gene's health then began to fail rapidly and he could no longer handle the steps. We bought a small townhouse in Stillwater, Minnesota through a strange series of events.

I had asked Ron Johnson to help me look at a one-level townhouse that I was interested in. He said "No." I couldn't believe it!

I said, "What do you mean, no. I thought you were our friend!" He replied, "I said no because you don't need to look at another townhouse. You're going to move next to us, so we can help you look after Gene."

Ron and Joan had recently bought a beautiful new townhouse in Stillwater, and there were still some units available, but I was concerned about cost for us. We looked at the units and decided to buy a smaller one on an inside street. It seemed ideal, and we signed the papers. Then the builder called twice with changes and we chose another similar unit, and then another.

During this time, we went to visit Joan and Ron whose back patio door opened on a beautiful small pond that was filled with wildlife. I saw the wistful look on Gene's face when he looked at that pond and silently prayed that we could have a similar view wherever we settled, even though all of the units on that pond were sold. The very next day at church, a woman friend who had bought the unit at the end of Johnson's building told me that she had cancelled her house and bought one in another development. I was stunned, but inwardly cheered. I immediately called the builder to see if it was still available. It was.

We moved in October and it was not a moment too soon. Gene's pain was increasing so that stairs were impossible now. Moving day was a hectic time with him hardly able to walk. In fact, he woke up that day in terrible pain and I didn't know how we could get through the day.

A miracle happened when I opened the door that morning to see the smiling faces of literally dozens of our wonderful Cursillo friends. They were there to work, and work they did, packing, hauling, and unpacking box after box.

By the end of the day Gene was settled in his recliner in the new house, already gazing at his beautiful pond and thanking God. Again, I prayed, "Please God, let him see all of the seasons on this lovely pond." And he did.

Goodbye to Gene

Shortly after Mom passed away, Gene signed himself on Hospice care in May of 2002. He was still able to walk, and feeling pretty good thanks to lots of pain medications, but we had been told by his doctors that there was no longer any treatment for his prostate bone cancer and that Hospice was the next step. This was a frightening time and we were both pretty numb from it all.

We talked over everything we had heard from the doctors and Gene made the decision to stop all of the "experimental" treatments that he'd been having for the past year or so. His hopes were raised and then plunged so many times that he just didn't want to go through this again. We talked with the Hospice people and were encouraged by the optimistic and cheerful attitude of the nurse assigned to Gene. At that time we had no idea of all of the wonderful people and care that were in store for both of us.

I had stopped travel for work and at this point began taking off an extra day a week to be home with Gene. What we didn't know was that Onno VanDemmeltraadt's wife Marjanne had also signed up for Hospice at the same time. She had an inherited form of Ataxia, called Machado Joseph's Disease, which was getting progressively worse. She was bed-ridden at that time and her doctors also advised Hospice.

Gene and Marjanne had some of the same Hospice workers and somehow during a session with her, one of the workers mentioned Gene's name.

Marjanne remembered him from church where the four of us knew each other slightly, and one day she phoned him just to chat. They both enjoyed their visit so much that they decided to keep in contact through the summer. Because Marjanne was not mobile, it was easier for her to do the calling at her convenience and they settled on Tuesday afternoons. The calls were simple and Gene told me that they talked about the birds and animals they could see from their respective windows, and the care they each received from the wonderful Hospice people and from their spouses. This became an eagerly anticipated part of Gene's week, along with Wednesdays when I was home, and other days with the Hospice nurse and our pastor coming to the house. Knowing how Gene enjoyed his conversations with Marjanne, I enquired about taking him to visit her in person, but this would have been too difficult for both of them and they were happy with their phone calls.

We lived in this comfortable and comforting place for one year and one month when it became evident that Gene was failing rapidly. After a series of short hospital stays, the Hospice people set up his bed in our living room so it would be easier to care for him. All of our children came from both coasts, North Dakota and throughout Minnesota, and dealing with the logistics of feeding and lodging everyone at that horrible time was made easier by wonderful friends and neighbors, for which I'll always be grateful.

For days, we played a silly game at the dining room table to keep us busy and there was much laughter that I know was comforting to Gene. Joan and Ron were there, too, and Joan had been organizing and coordinating food for everyone at the house for at least two weeks. Her gentle presence was like lotion on chapped hands for all of us, and along with the wonderful Hospice staff and many friends, we were well cared for.

Gene breathed his last on November 19, 2002, with his loving family around him. His passing was as quiet and calm as his life, and our friend Pat said so beautifully, "Gene taught us all how to die with dignity."

15. Gene and Gloria with all 6 children:
Lee, Karen, Paul, Greg, Renee, and Mark in July 2002.

Chapter 6

The end and the beginning

After Gene died, my physical self was in a mess as well as my mental state. I had gained a lot of weight due to inactivity and poor eating for the past several years, and that made me feel even worse. I knew that change was needed and because there wasn't much else to do, I began to basically move more and eat less. I joined Curves for Women and worked out every morning before work. I began to crave vegetables and fruits that had been absent from my diet for too long. Before long, the weight fell off and I lost about 40 pounds. I got back to what must be my "normal" weight because I've have stayed there for almost seven years. I continue to work out often and I do eat much healthier than I used to, and I feel better than I have ever felt.

In the summer of 2003, I began a period of extreme loneliness and unhappiness with my life, my work, and just about everything else. I missed Gene and felt guilty because I would get angry that he died and left me alone. I went to visit Lee and Sara in Oregon, and Lee said, "Mom, maybe it's time for you to look for somebody. I think you need someone in your life and maybe this is the time." I was shocked to hear him say this, but the more I thought about it, the more I knew he was right. But, how to do it? How does one go looking for another mate after 33 years of comfortable compatibility with someone else? This was scary!

Meanwhile, as I learned later, Onno was going through the same sort of misery. He had gone to Holland after Marjanne's death in March 2003, when she peacefully slipped away. He visited friends and family for a couple of months, and when it came time to go home, he was confused and lonely, and had a conversation with God. He said, "Okay God, I don't know what I want, but I do know what I don't want. What I don't want is to grow old alone—you have to find someone for me. I'm confident that you will show me the way and bring the right woman for me. I expect that this will take at least a couple of years, maybe two and a half, so let's start." And off he went, home to Lake Elmo.

It has been said that if you want to make God laugh, give Him your timetable. Well, God must have been chuckling, because less than two weeks later, Onno and I were standing in the midst of a group of women at church. Someone said, "I miss Marjanne," and I heard Onno say, "Yes, I miss her, too." Then someone else said to me, "I miss Gene," and I gave the same answer. There was more chatter and someone was talking about email, and Onno looked at me and said, "Remember, I have email, too."

For the rest of the day, I couldn't get the sad look on Onno's face out of my mind. I kept thinking of a way to make him feel better, so when I was sending notes via email to my children that afternoon, I sent a quick note to Onno, saying that it was good to see him back at church and I hoped he was doing okay. Surprisingly, I got a reply back right away with a delightfully funny comment and his Dutch accent and humor came through loud and clear. We emailed back and forth for the rest of that day, and thus it all began.

Later, I found out that Onno checked his email only about every two weeks or so. It just happened that we were both on line at the same time that afternoon.

After many emails and phone calls, the first time we got together was for Onno to give me a tennis lesson. I had never played tennis and he's been an expert for most of his life, so we decided that I could learn. On a Sunday afternoon at the end of August, I met him on the tennis court at his house, and the lessons began.

With much laughter and nervousness on my part, I learned how to hold a racquet and hit the ball. I learned something else that day, too, and that was how carefully Onno's friends were watching over him.

We were barely into the basics of the game, when a man walked onto the court. It was Hendrik, Onno's good friend. He and his wife Marsha were helping the next door neighbor and just happened to see us on the court, so of course Hendrik had to check out the woman with Onno.

After the tennis lesson I learned that Onno had been invited to his friends' and neighbors' Toni and Dexter Ziton, for an afternoon of fun by the lake. Of course, they had told Onno to bring me with him.

Years later, Toni, who is now one of my closest friends, described this day in the perfect way—she called it "a magic day." And magic it was. After a lively time of hitting a tennis ball for the first time, and seeing first hand Onno's patience and kindness, off we went to a rousing gathering of dozens of exuberant and joyful people.

It was mainly the Ziton family, plus some close friends, and they were celebrating the end of summer and just being together and having a good time. I barely knew Toni and Dexter from church and the others were all new to me. But not for long. I had a wonderful time getting to know a whole new group of fascinating people, most of whom were of Lebanese background. We ate unknown to me, but delicious Lebanese foods, like Kibby and Tabouli. The recipes provided are "generic," according to Toni because "If Dexter gave you his real recipes, he'd have to kill you!" It seems that even their kids don't have the real recipes and they have to learn them by watching their dad, but these are pretty good.

Recipe: Tabouli,
Recipe: Kibby
Recipe: Green Beans and Lamb

As Onno and I determined later, this magic day was the beginning of both of us wanting to know each other better. We also knew that this wasn't the only "magic" in our getting together. We remember the phone calls that Gene and Marjanne so enjoyed during their summer on Hospice care, and we wonder more and more if they, along with God in heaven, had anything to do with that meeting. The way we both felt that day in church at the moment we made eye contact was so remarkable, I wouldn't call it "magic," I'd call it "blessed."

16. Vallee de Croix Chorus (Gloria's on the right end, middle row)

Soon after Onno and I began seeing each other, I had a trip to Phoenix with the Sweet Adelines. I had joined this wonderful singing group shortly after Gene passed away, and I was thoroughly enjoying learning to sing barbershop music. The Vallee de Croix Chapter had won the regional contest prior to my joining the chorus, and I was lucky enough to be included in the international competition in Phoenix.

I think that Onno was trying to impress me because he insisted that in addition to driving me to the airport the morning I left for Phoenix, that he wanted to make a special breakfast for me. To be honest, breakfast was the last thing I wanted to think about that morning what with packing, leaving my cat, getting away from work, and getting ready for a big trip. This whole relationship was new and a little scary, but he was so nice and wanted to do something for me, so I thought, "Hey, this man cooks—how great is that?!"

I came speeding up his driveway that morning, late of course, and there he was, with a beautiful sweet smelling stack of crepes. There was fruit, juice and all sorts of things to put on the crepes and they really were delicious. He did the job—I was very impressed. What I learned later was that crepes are Onno's entire cooking repertoire! He does make wonderful coffee, and terrific reservations, but that's the extent of his culinary abilities. We laugh about his sneaky way to get my attention, and now he says that we split the kitchen duties 50-50; I cook and he eats!

Recipe: (Breakfasts) Crepes

It's truly amazing how life has changed for me. From not being able to cook at all, I've come full circle. I cook more now in later years than ever before and I love it. It started with a trip to Elly Mettler's and the whole bunch of Indo folks who were eager to meet the woman who captured their beloved Onno's attention.

First, let's learn about what I described as "Indo folks." This is the briefest of descriptions, but it might help a little. Onno was born in the Dutch East Indies, as were a huge share of his friends, relatives, and acquaintances. The islands now known as Indonesia (more than 15,000 of them) were known as the "Spice Islands" in our American textbooks, and were a colony of Holland.

It wasn't until after WWII that Indonesia became independent. This was a terrible period during which Sukarno ruled and thousands of Dutch and European people were slaughtered. Survivors were forced to flee, mostly to Holland, and Indonesia was established.

Good or bad, Holland had governed the East Indies for at least 200 years, and in addition to a supportive lifestyle for the indigenous people, there was a flourishing and prosperous Dutch culture there. It was common for Dutch and other European men to join with local women and have families, thus beginning the generations of part Dutch/European, part Indonesian people.

In later years they started to call themselves "Indo," referring to this mixture. The term "Indo" at one time was a less-than acceptable slang term, but it has gained acceptance and some pride through the years. A few full Dutch people born in what they still call the Dutch East Indies even call themselves Indo also, because of their deep love for their country of birth.

During World War II, Japan occupied the Dutch East Indies. Many atrocities occurred during this time and life was very hard for the Dutch/Europeans. At the beginning of the war, each person was evaluated for how much of their heritage was not native, and they were given a number as to when they would have to enter the prison camps. Onno's father, along with thousands of others, was forced into prison camp immediately, and his successful automobile/motorcycle dealership was confiscated. All bank accounts were confiscated also.

Onno, along with his brother Huibert and their mother Erna, were forced to live wherever they could, like others of any Dutch or European heritage. Many people had to share houses or apartments. When the business was confiscated, Onno's mother went to the hospital with an asthma attack, and the children were sent to live with a relative. When she got better, the three of them went to live with Erna's brother and sister, Om (Uncle) Ben, and Tante (Aunt) Marie. The family's life story from this time period is incredibly fascinating, but too complicated and special to explain briefly in this manuscript. I will only peak your curiosity here, for a future narrative.

Interestingly, Onno's parents had built a beautiful new home in the mountains above the city of Bandung on the island of Java. The new house was almost ready and the family was scheduled to move into it the very week of the start of the war. Onno tells the story of his father on the way to the new house with the silver, when he heard many loud sirens and gunfire, and he fled back to the city. He left the silver, which included many plates and serving pieces as well as dinnerware, with someone on the way and never remembered who that was. The silver was lost of course, but it very likely supported many people through the war if it was sold off in pieces.

Onno's mother was able to sell off furniture, rugs, and other valuables from the new house to help them survive the war, also, but the house itself was lost. The family never did live in it, and it eventually became a school for the area.

Back to the food. This is a hugely important element of life to the Indos. Not just food to survive as it is to many. Not at all. I have learned that food was and is a combination of smells and tastes and textures to be enjoyed, nay, to be *savored*. As Onno comically, but seriously put it during an early conversion between the two of us, "There are only so many meals left on this earth, and they had better all be good!" As you can imagine, I was more than nervous about my first foray to unknown territory, that is, the first invitation to try this new stuff. Hence, off we went to Elly's.

Oh boy was I surprised! I can't remember everything we ate that night, but it was all new to me—and delicious! There was **gado gado** (Indonesian salad) **chicken sate**, with **peanut sauce**, **krupuk** (shrimp crackers) **babi ketjap** (pork in sweet soy sauce) **nasi goreng** (fried rice) **sambal goreng kentang** (sweet and spicy shoestring potatoes) and more. I couldn't believe how wonderful everything tasted, and I loved the spiciness of it all.

Recipes: Gado GadoChicken Sate
Peanut Sauce
Krupuk
Babi Ketjap
Nasi Goreng
Sambal Goreng Kentang

The vegetables were the most surprising and delicious aspect of this meal. My vegetable world to this point included peas and carrots and green beans, and not much more. When I was little, my mom would put a can of peas in a pot and boil them for 10 minutes. She would then pour those tiny grey tasteless lumps, water and all, into a bowl and that was the meal's vegetable.

Now I was faced with fresh and crisp bok choy, Chinese cabbage, bean sprouts, and more. All were cooked to perfection in sauces and spices that enhanced each of them. They not only peaked my palate, but inspired a penchant for recreating these tastes at home.

What made it all even better was the wonderful reception of these beautiful gentle people. We went to the home of Elly and Ron Mettler, and also there were Marsha and Hendrik Celosse, Bepe and Roeland Ryers, and Sandy and Frans Officer. Of this group, Onno, Hendrik, Ron, and Frans are partly Indonesian, all born in The Dutch East Indies, plus Roeland, who is full Dutch, was born there, too, and considers himself Indo also.

An interesting aside is that Onno and Hendrik both grew up in the city of Bandung on the island of Java, and very near each other. They didn't know each other there, but met on the tennis court in St. Paul when both had eventually moved to Minnesota after separate adventures all over the world, and were working for the 3M Company.

Together with Onno

Onno and I were married January 24, 2004. It was a whirlwind courtship, but we both seemed to know very soon that "this was it." I was very apprehensive at first. Onno was persistent and so convinced that this was the right thing from the beginning, that it was almost scary. I talked about my uncertainties with a friend at work who said, "Gloria, the brass ring only comes around once. Grab it!"

This was only a month or so after our first meeting, when my daughter Karen sent a precious email. I was nervous about my first real dinner date. She replied with this loving advice, "Just enjoy the dinner out and each other's company. If there's a kiss goodnight, go home and cry for what was, and smile for what's to come." That's exactly what I did, and from that point on I never looked back.

When I told Onno about Karen's sweet message, I also told him that I had never kissed a man with a mustache, so even that was new. He said, "Well, there's an old Dutch saying," (I've since learned that there's an old Dutch saying that applies to just about every situation in life, according to Onno . . .) "A kiss without a mustache is like an egg without salt."

I retired from my job the week of the wedding. I had reservations about quitting work and considered working part time for a while, but Onno convinced me that it was time to walk away. I did, and I've never looked back. I was 62 years old and ready for a totally new life. It has surely been that!

17. Gloria and Onno toasting the wedding, January 24, 2004.

We had a fun and people-filled wedding at our church in Lake Elmo. Our dear friend Pastor Jerry Malak presided and the wedding included both of our families with children, grandchildren, nieces and nephews, and more. There were lots of other friends and relatives, plus many church people, Hospice workers, and gals from my Sweet Adelines chorus. It was a joyous event with tears and laughter, and prayers for happiness that meant the world to both of us.

Food was a key part of the whole wedding adventure, from a lovely engagement party at Bruce and Cassie Tyler's, to the rehearsal dinner the night before the wedding. That was a delicious catered dinner at the church for family and friends, and a time for many in our blending families to meet each other. Because we had issued so many open invitations, we had no idea how many people would come to the wedding itself, so we had just coffee, cake, punch, and bars, and the gracious ladies of the church served it.

We took a beautiful honeymoon cruise to the Panama Canal, which was eye-opening for me because I had hardly been out of the U.S. Of course, you eat yourself silly on any cruise, and we weren't an exception. The ship's food was amazing.

The Panama Canal was awesome to see, and we took several side trips at ports on the way. One adventure took us far into the jungle to a native village. We spent an afternoon with the people and they cooked a simple meal for us that included fish wrapped in banana leaves, and fried plantain.

Recipe: Bananas, Fried

Back to Reality in Frozen Minnesota

I moved into Onno's house and we eventually sold my townhouse. Moving was pretty awful with having to squeeze in my houseful of "stuff" along with Onno's already too full house. We rented a dumpster and got rid of a lot, but alas, our treasures were plentiful and parting with them was difficult. As my daughter Renee said, "Gloria, moving is not your forte." Thankfully, our families helped this process along.

We did some planned updating of the kitchen, and remodeled the basement after a frozen sewer pipe disaster that happened while we were on our honeymoon cruise. We've painted and decorated throughout the house, and Onno made me happy by giving me the extra bedroom next to his office to use as my office/den/craft room. It's a terrible mess constantly, but it's a place to store my craft supplies, work on my computer (we each have one and that was a major indulgence, but we're worth it) and sew, and I love it.

The yard is major work with many levels of terraces and walls, and we've done a lot of landscaping and plantings of flowers and shrubbery. It's a great place for us for now, and we'll stay here for as long as we can take care of the place. After that, who knows?

Day to day life with each other continues to be an unfolding flower of beauty for both Onno and me. We don't tire of each other's company even being together day and night, which is a source of wonder for me.

We start the day early with coffee and then do our daily Bible reading, which we decided to do at the beginning of our marriage. This was a first for me, and we started on page 1 of Genesis. We try to read a chapter a day, but we miss some days because of travel and such. And, some days we get so wrapped up in a paragraph, or a story, or even just a sentence, that we start talking, arguing, laughing, and living what we're reading, that it takes several days to read a chapter.

At this point, we're just finishing up the Book of Acts. When we reach the end of Revelation, I expect that we'll start from the beginning again. By that time we'll have a whole new collection of memories and experiences that will apply to what we're reading, and will make it yet another fresh event.

Family

Our children and grandchildren give us much joy. It's hard to have many of them far away so that we can't see them often, but through the miracle of cell phones, email, webcams, and the like, we keep tabs on all of them. I am proud of the people my children have become, in the responsible way they live their lives, the partners they've chosen, and the strong work ethics all have demonstrated. Above all, I am thrilled and humbled to see the way they share their hearts with those they love.

A great recipe that Onno has learned to cook since we've been together is fried tofu, or tahu as it's called in Indonesia. Tofu is something that I tried once years ago to disastrous results and never ate again until meeting Onno. We sprang this treat on my unsuspecting family by calling it tahu so they wouldn't know what it was. It sounded exotic and everybody tried it just to "fit in" with the rest of the gang. To everyone's surprise, they loved the crunchy garlicky taste, and now it's a whole family favorite that Onno loves to prepare when we have a few family members at our house—like 30 or so.

Recipe: (Appetizers) Tofu

Besides seeing our families whenever we can, Onno and I are busy with volunteer activities for church, Hospice, and elsewhere. While I was busy for several years doing marketing things and writing press releases for the Vallee de Croix Sweet Adelines chorus, I've had to leave the chorus because of hearing problems. I miss the people and the music, but the stress of trying to hear and the impossibility of blending tones while wearing a hearing aid is gone, and my hours are already filled with new adventures.

We continue to experiment in the kitchen and Onno likes my cooking more and more. I'm having a fun time learning about new tastes and smells. I've never really had time to cook before, so I am thoroughly enjoying this new experience. And, Onno does his share of cooking, too—like I said before, he makes great reservations!

Chapter 7

Travels

Traveling has been wonderful fun with Onno, and in the short time we've been together, we have gone to Holland, Indonesia, Hawaii, the East and West US Coasts, Branson, Missouri, Florida, and a whole lot of places in between. We've traveled several times with Bonthy and Bertje Kiliaan from Holland, and we have great cribbage tournaments. Bonthy and Onno were friends as children in Indonesia, and they share a love of Indonesian and Dutch foods.

Briefly, here are some experiences, recipes and meals from some of our travels, in a sort of sequential order:

Holland

Yes, it is officially named The Netherlands, but whether because of affection for their country, or convenience in syllables, current and former residents still refer to it as Holland. We went there for a month in April/May 2004, on my maiden trip to Europe. My senses were overwhelmed with new experiences. From the architecture to the landscapes to the foods, I soaked it up like gravy into bread. I loved it all!

The tiny country of Holland is one-seventh the size of Minnesota, and has more than twice as many people. And they *all* ride bicycles! Roads are narrow with almost no shoulders, so driving is daunting to say the least. In addition to dodging the bicycles, cars and trucks drive fast and very close together. Our US "rule" of leaving so much space between vehicles is unheard of, and as we hurtled around the country in our rental car, with one narrow escape after another, I was convinced that only prayer allowed us to make it home unscathed.

We stayed with a number of Onno's friends and relatives throughout the trip, so my new experiences were many and varied.

As might be expected in a small country with a large population, houses are tall and narrow. Two and three stories high, they have tiny, well-kept gardens in front and back, as opposed to our sprawling American homes surrounded by acres of grass. Each home's front garden demonstrates the owner's individuality and creativity in a tiny space, and there is much pride evident in their creations.

The tall and narrow theme carries through in the cities as well, with buildings close together and appearing to teeter on the edge of the canals that course through the metropolitan areas.

In the ocean-front city of Noordwyk I discovered the Dutch **Kroket**, a delicious treat that is meat in a thick potato paste, rolled in crumbs and deep fried. Also, the **sozyse-broodje**, which is a delicious sausage biscuit—and the first word I learned in Dutch. Both of these are sold in busy little sidewalk bakeries and it looked like everyone was walking down the street munching on one or the other.

I learned to eat **toasted sesame seeds on peanut butter toast** at Aaf and Jan Schneyder's house—delicious (Jan is Onno's deceased wife Marjanne's brother).

Anja is Marjanne's sister and we had great Dutch food at her house. I learned about **white asparagus**, which is the only kind of asparagus that the Dutch will eat. It is grown underground and the earth is piled on top of the growing spears in rows to keep the sun from hitting them. You peel the stalks first, then boil the white asparagus gently, and serve with butter sauce. Anja also fed us **red cabbage**, boiled with onion, salt and pepper.

We went to dinner with Anja on Easter Sunday 2004 at a restaurant in a 350 year-old cottage in the middle of a deep forest. The dinner was the most elegant and formal that I've ever had. There was fish for the main course and with it was a single large white asparagus spear. The appetizer was thin sliced lamb with pine nuts and lettuces, plus quail soup and the most wonderful desert I ever ate. It was a soft delicate meringue with spun sugar on top and a wonderful sweet sauce and little pasta squares filled with chocolate paste. Amazing!

For this dinner as well as for most meals throughout the country, we had tiny cups of strong coffee with milk, and always a chocolate or other small sweet with the coffee—a great tradition from my perspective!

Bonthy, Onno's life-long friend and his wife Bertje, live in Northern Holland, in the province of Friesland. Both are wonderful cooks, and they made us **sate with peanut sauce, gado gado and nasi goreng,** all delicious foods that were so new to me and so comforting to Onno. We stayed several days with the Kiliaans and saw much of the area.

The main motivation for this trip to Holland was for Onno to attend the 50th reunion of his college fraternity, called Kattebak. Along with Bonthy and Bertje, we traveled by car to the south of Holland to the tiny village of Margraten, very near the border of Belgium, for this gathering.

We stayed in a charming small hotel, and actually our group of 25 took over the whole hotel. It was great fun to watch this select group of accomplished and distinguished men instantly revert to a gaggle of wise-cracking 18-year-old boys. Bonthy was a clear leader of the pack. They played jokes on each other and drank lots of beer, and there was lots of laughter. I chatted with the other wives and enjoyed getting to know them. Fortunately, this group spoke English very well. Through it all it, was obvious how much they cared about each other, and the entire get-together was heart-warming.

We toured the area by bus with this group, and it was interesting to see so many hills, as the majority of Holland is very flat. We also went on an adventure into the limestone caves of that area where American and British pilots were hidden during WWII.

The caves were very deep with many miles of hidden trails. I heard the guide say there were 250 kilometers of underground trails. Of course, the guide spoke Dutch, so I didn't understand much, but I learned later that the caves produced tons and tons of limestone that continued to be mined through the war to use in buildings.

Because of the cold and dampness of the caves, a person could not stay in the depths of the caverns for more than 72 hours at a time, or they would develop hypothermia and die. This made it necessary for allies who hid the pilots to bring them above ground periodically, and they used the mining noise and confusion to cover their clandestine activities.

As our group stumbled through the cold and damp tunnels in the caves, with only two small lanterns to light our way in the complete blackness, it was both frightening and awesome. It was frightening to imagine finding the way and somehow living for weeks in such utter darkness. And awesome to think of the dangers and sacrifices made by so many to save the lives of complete strangers.

It was a somber, cold, and shivering assembly that gratefully emerged from the frigid caves and welcomed the sunshine.

Further tours throughout Holland took us to the city of Gouda and we toured a factory where the famous Delft blue pottery is made. Of course, we bought many pieces to take home as gifts.

We crossed the Afsluitdijk, a 19-mile long dike that was recently completed. The Dutch have been reclaiming land from the sea for more than 2000 years, and their expertise in dikes and windmills is remarkable to see. Always practical, local farmers use the green grass on the steeply sided dikes to graze their sheep.

Another sobering moment was a tour through the Museum Bronbeek in the city of Arnhem. This is the oldest museum in Holland and it contains artifacts, cannon, and statuary depicting events and the aftermath of WWII in the former Dutch East Indies.

Onno had told me a little of their family's experiences during the war, but this tour underscored the agonies suffered by everyone during this terrible time. Most captions were written in Dutch, but the pictures were graphic enough to move me to tears as I began to understand what hardships were endured. Onno, in his eternally optimistic way, had only shared his good memories and the trip to Bronbeek was a startling awakening for me.

All in all, this journey through Holland was remarkable. It was filled with new and fresh experiences, including sights, and sounds, and tastes, that have forever altered my view of life.

I cherish these memories and they encourage me to experiment with foods that were unknown to me for more than half a century. As Onno says, "All of my life I've been surrounded by beautiful women who cook." What more encouragement could I ask for?

Branson, Missouri

October 2004: We took a fun trip in Onno's old blue van, and Bonthy and Bertje came from Holland to join us. We drove through miles and miles of cornfields in Iowa and the Dutch folks loved it!

There are so many people in the tiny and crowded country of Holland that there are no vast fields of grain as there are in the U.S. They have a different perspective on what could be perceived as a "boring" trip to others!

We went to the Grotto of the Redemption in West Bend, Iowa. I've been there before, and it was fun to see the reaction of these new folks at seeing the amazing work of love that one dedicated priest accomplished with semi-precious stones and a lot of work; a huge tribute to Christ in the Stations of the Cross, all built with stones.

On to Branson, Missouri, where we saw some terrific shows and attractions like Shojo Tabuchi, a famous violinist, and Ann Margret and Andy Williams, and Silver Dollar City.

We drove on to St. Louis and went to the top of the Arch; 630 feet high and wide. It was scary as it swayed slightly in the wind, and truly awesome!

On the way home, we went to a little-known tourist attraction in Marshalltown, Iowa, that is known as the world's biggest tree house. The grandmother of the man for whom the tree house was built gave us a tour of the 12-level high structure that is indeed built into an enormous maple tree. It has running water, lots of swings, hidey holes, TVs, and resting places. There are beautiful plantings and flowers all around, and it is a unique and interesting thing to see.

Food on this trip was pretty mundane except for one great breakfast. Near Hannibal, Missouri, we watched a barge enter a lock on the Mississippi River, and we talked with a man who was going fishing with his buddies. He told us that his wife was a great cook in a new motel nearby. Needing a place to stay for the night, we decided to try it and he was right. We had a great breakfast of fresh and wholesome foods, after a comfortable night's sleep. It almost made up for an unpleasant experience in a real "fleabag" motel the night before!

Indonesia

Onno and I went to Indonesia in January 2005 for a reunion of anyone who had ever attended the same Christian school in the city of Bandung on the island of Java.

Class members of this school refer to themselves as the Vedo group and they currently have an active email connection where they share stories and memories. The Vedo group was instrumental in planning and organizing the reunion.

18. Gloria in Indonesia with a group of boys just leaving their soccer practice, January 2005.

There were more than 125 people in Bandung for a week of festivities that were well planned and exciting. After the reunion, we went on a three-week bus trip, a tour of the island of Java. There were 70 folks in two buses, all of whom spoke Dutch except for me. I insert here a piece that I wrote about my first impressions of Indonesia, which I was asked to do by the people we traveled with on the trip.

First-Timer Impressions of Indonesia (written in 2005)

I met and married Onno VanDemmeltraadt only one year ago. Prior to that time I have lived in Minnesota in the north-central part of the U.S. for all of my life, and until last year, have never traveled outside of the country. This trip to Indonesia has been a remarkable, wonderful, and overwhelming experience that I will treasure for the rest of my life.

There have been tears—for the people living in crowded muddy huts in flooded areas of Jakarta, and when I look into faces filled with desperation among the poor along our journey. And, there has been much laughter, to see happy children at play in their simple but loved surroundings, with the caring closeness of families working and living together.

The vast number of people has been shocking—there are hordes of people everywhere—walking, squatting along the roads just watching the traffic, riding motorcycles, working in fields, pressuring tourists and others to buy their wares, trying to make a living any way they can. But I am impressed by their industriousness, well kept fields, and their struggles to keep things clean in spite of poverty, little technology, and the humid tropical climate.

All of the shades of green are beautiful. As one man said, "You can shove any stick in the ground here and it will grow." The palm trees, ferns, spice plants, and endless watery rice fields climbing up and down the mountains, are breathtaking.

I love the many varieties of fruits that I never heard of before—salak is my favorite. It's like a cross between an apple and a pear, crisp and sweet, with three sections that each have a large seed. I've tried everything, and have enjoyed almost every new dish served.

The mountains are spectacular. Among the most impressive tours was a walk on an active volcano to its boiling caldera of molten lava. We got as close as the heat would allow. Scalding water spurted from the rocks around us, and steam rose from it all, making it a surreal and awesome experience. I've since learned that there are 151 active volcanoes in Indonesia (the most in the world), and earthquakes are common.

We had tours of several ancient Buddhist and Hindu temples, and this made me feel very small, indeed, when I thought of all the feet that climbed those very steps over many centuries.

There are fewer flowers than I expected, but I see that there are more useful fruit trees planted instead. Food is of the utmost importance, and seems to be in abundance. Every inch of space is used for growing food or something useful. Personal living surroundings are secondary and are not kept up.

Maintenance seems to be non-existent. Ceramic tile floors are swept, but not much else is done to preserve buildings. Roofs are not repaired or replaced, and I made the observation that when the roof wears out, whether it's a house, hotel, school, or business, the building just collapses. It's sad to see.

The garbage situation is appalling. There seem to be no laws or provisions for garbage and people just toss it over the fence and out of sight for them. Every house and every village has its personal pile of rubbish trailing down to the canal and in full view of the roads.

The canal system is impressive. It is moving water, brown-red in color, likely because of the iron in the soil, and is basically a sewer into which all of the waste water empties from houses and villages. The canals parallel the roads, and many times on our way by in the bus, we saw people squatting in the canal to do their daily business, and just down the way was someone else taking a bath.

The water is diverted and pumped into the rice fields in a fascinating pathway where it is gravity driven to flood each "sawa," or rice paddy, and dribble down to the next. Some of the canals looked like they were built, and some were natural streams or rivers. There is water everywhere, but even the locals don't drink it. Our hotels supplied bottled water for drinking and brushing teeth, and signs were everywhere warning to not drink the water.

We had a wonderful tour through a small village (kampong) as the people went about their daily routine. We walked the hard-packed dirt of the village among happy children, chickens, and cats. We saw people there making coconut sugar (gula jawa) out of liquid collected from the flowers atop the coconut trees. It was delicious!

We watched a man who was carving puppets for the Wayang plays. He said that it took seven years to learn about all of the characters and to perform the plays, which are fascinating stories of royal figures. The plays sometimes last for several evenings, with many characters played by one person.

There were women doing the laundry—scrubbing it by hand—with well water hauled up in buckets. There was a gentle and serene feeling in the village, and the people were quietly doing what they've done for generations, providing their living from day to day.

We went through a "cottage industry" clay pottery business, another that makes krupuk (shrimp crackers), one that makes tofu from soybeans, and visited a silver shop that produces beautiful hand-made silver items. We also watched the process of making batik fabric, with many people applying the wax by stamping it or by hand with tiny applicators for intricate designs. No OSHA laws here, and many of the processes were quite dangerous.

The Gamelan and Anklung music is fascinating and the Ramayana and Wayang plays and dancing are beautiful. The people exhibit many advanced artistic talents, yet maintain a humble demeanor. For example, our plantation guide in Kalibaru spoke perfect English, had an extensive knowledge of every process, plant, and activity on the plantation, and appeared to be well educated and professional. The same man later quietly served and cleared our plates at dinner.

It has been difficult to understand everything and not speaking Dutch or Indonesian is a handicap, but people have been very thoughtful to interpret for me. My few Dutch words have not been too helpful (Oliphant and sozyse-broodje . . .) and we've all had fun with that, but I hope my efforts with the language improve with time and Onno's patience.

One of the greatest joys for me on this trip has been to watch the happiness and nostalgic emotions of the people of the Vedo group. They truly love Indonesia and loved this opportunity to relive their memories. I have gained new insight into my husband's personality, and now I better understand how his gentle character and nature were formed by his early years in this country. I am humbly grateful to have made this trip, and will remember and share my experiences for years to come.

East Coast

In July 2005, my eldest son Greg, his wife Lori, and their son Ian in Germantown, Maryland, made us breakfast of **Spinach Soufflé** that was wonderful! Greg and Lori love to cook together in the kitchen and produce many "gourmet" meals.

Onno's cousin Corrie near Williamsburg, VA is a wonderful Dutch/Indonesian cook and we had great **saté** there. Corrie also gave me many tips on Indo cooking and ways of using spices, like mace and nutmeg, that are new to me.

In Utica, Michigan, we saw another cousin of Onno's, Ina and her husband Han Lysse, and their family. Ina gave me the wonderful recipe for **Candied Pecans**, that I've made and given as gifts to many. She also gave me her recipe for **Soto, Chinese Chicken Soup** that is delicious.

While at their home, I discovered the beautiful book, "*Memoirs of an Indo Woman*," written by Marguerite Skenkhauzen (Mother of Doeschka, wife of Onno's cousin Humphrey). Ina let me take it home to finish reading this wonderful, stark, and severe story that fills in many of the gaps in the fascinating history I've learned about Onno's childhood in Indonesia. Sadly, Ina was diagnosed with lung cancer and passed away in 2007.

Oregon

November 2005: Henry Lee Cannon was born on November 4, 2005 to my son Lee and his wife Sara, and Onno and I were thrilled to visit when Henry was still really tiny. We've had more trips to Oregon since then, and have enjoyed some great meals that Sara puts together. She's a wonderful cook, with Greta's help, of course. Here's their recipe for **chocolate beet cake** that pleased the crowd for Henry's 3rd birthday in 2008, and we've had salmon tacos, and oven baked vegetables drizzled with balsamic vinegar that were terrific.

Trips to the west coast usually include a visit to Onno's brother, Huibert and his wife Judy, in nearby Washington, and Huibert's daughter Margie and her husband Wayne, and sons Sam and Matt, are there, too. We stay at both Lee and Sara's house in Portland and their beautiful mountain place in Lyle, Washington. Both Lee and Sara love to windsurf and they are close to the world's best windsurfing on the Columbia River Gorge.

Alaska

June 2006: We booked a fabulous Alaskan cruise and land tour, along with Bonthy and Bertje Kiliaan, who came from Holland and spent some with us in Minnesota before and after the trip. We did the land tour first, on the advice of others who said that it was really tiring and it's good to relax on the ship at the end of the trip. They were right.

We first flew to Fairbanks, where the sun was shining brightly at almost midnight. It's hard to sleep when it's still dazzling outside, but we managed.

Our trip was full of many adventures, including a bus tour of Denali National Park, which is huge and starkly beautiful. We saw bears and moose, eagles, and deer. We took the "Devil's Canyon Adventure," with a bus to Talkeetna and boarded a jet boat for a whole day on the Susitna river. Sights included immense panoramas of snow-topped mountains, endless prairies, and many animals. We even panned for gold, and of course found several tiny nuggets.

While on the river, a young moose suddenly appeared and was swimming for a while beside our boat, before turning toward shore and running off into the brush. The guide said this was unusual and not good. In his experience, he knew that the half-grown moose would not survive if he was on his own as it appeared that he was. He sadly said that this little guy would likely become lunch for a grizzly bear.

For five days we traveled by train, bus, and boat south toward Anchorage. There, we eventually boarded a Princess line ship, and relaxed through a luxurious seven-day cruise of the Inside Passage. Views of Glacier Bay were awesome, and we took several side trips, including an adventure deep in the woods to a glacier lake. We thought we were dressed warm enough, but each got extra jackets and boots from the tour guides, and we really needed them.

We paddled in canoes on the freezing lake out toward a glacier. We couldn't get too close in fear of huge blocks of ice that could suddenly burst up out of the water and easily capsize a small boat. It was exciting and awe-inspiring, and also menacing to see a monstrous wall of ice towering above you, with enormous slabs breaking off with no warning and landing with a huge splash in the water below.

19. Bertje, Bonthy, Onno and Gloria in Alaska, June 2006.

At the end of the cruise, the four of us stayed an extra day or so in Vancouver, British Columbia, to relax after an action-packed adventure in Alaska. We did a lot of walking around the city and particularly liked the area called "Gastown" where we heard the deep whooshing sound of the world's first steam-powered clock.

Hawaii

Onno and I went to Hawaii in the spring of 2007. In fact Dexter took us to the airport on February 28, in the midst of the sort of winter for which Minnesota is known. We had had snow for several days and my shoulders were aching from shoveling it. There were worries that our flight might be cancelled due to snow as were many other flights, but we were lucky and took off on time.

It was eight hours to Honolulu and another hour to Hilo, landing in welcome warmth and luscious green, green, green. The lushness was like Minnesota house plants gone huge, and they were set amid tall swaying palm trees and vibrant jungle flowers. It was enormously beautiful.

We had wonderful visits in Hilo with my sister Fran and her family, and spent a lot of the time just hanging out at Frannie's house. Eleven years older than I, Fran and I grew up in different worlds and we never really knew each other very well. After more than 50 years of minimal contact, this visit was a wonderful regeneration of our relationship.

We talked about family memories, and got comfortable with each other after many years apart. Fran and Onno bonded right away, and we all shared many stories about our life experiences.

It rained a lot—even more than usual, from our understanding. I saw a sign in downtown Hilo, saying, "Welcome to Hilo, the rainiest city in America!" It was a good thing that we had family to see, or the rain could definitely have dampened our spirits.

In spite of the rain, we had a great time. We went to a planetarium exhibit on Mauna Kea volcano that was really interesting. Prior to the exhibit we had lunch and ate ono, a great Hawaiian fish. Ono means "delicious" in Hawaiian, and it was surely that.

When we had a wonderful family dinner at Fran's daughter Susan's house, Susan gave me her recipe for **Butter Mochi**, a terrific rice flour cake. Fran's wonderful diverse and hospitable family treated us to delicious Korean cooking which is mainly lots of spicy vegetables and little meat. We loved the fresh fruits growing there, including my favorite mangos.

We left Hilo for the Kona side of the Big Island and had a good time there—at least we had a little sunshine. On the way we went to Henk and Akemi's home at Puuwaauoa Ranch. Henk is a cousin of our friend Hendrik Celosse and he has a beautiful spot that was part of an original 100,000 acre ranch. They have the initial 100 year-old house and it is grand with an amazing view for many miles to the sea. Henk and Akemi had a wonderful gathering of Indo folks they know in the area, and along with about 16-20 people we had a typical Indo feast, and a day of fascinating chatter.

20. Hawaii 2007, Susan, Frances, Curtis, Gloria, and Rhea.

We flew to the island of Kauai and among many wonderful adventures there, we drove to Waimea Canyon. This was a spectacular sight of deep valleys and craggy mountains. The mountains have layers of different colored rock and the red rock and soil runs through it like veins of rich blood. There were many waterfalls collecting the recent rains and they united in fury and plummeted over the red rock to the river far below. We learned that the center of the mountains—the other side of Waimea Canyon—is the rainiest spot on earth, and it is so remote that no one can go there. It is an authentic rain forest where people cannot go to destroy God's creation.

On Kauai, we relaxed with our coffee and Bible reading in the mornings as at home, and we even found a tennis court for a short time of volleying balls.

We toured the Koloa and Poipu areas in the South of the island, and we saw Spouting Horn. This is a hole in the lava shelf where the sea waves push through and cause a high plume of spray high into the air. There was also an eerie sound when the surf crashed into the hole. A beautiful and peculiar sight.

Back in Honolulu, we toured Pearl Harbor, an impressive and somber place. It must have been low tide because we could see more of the ghostly sunken battleship, Arizona, than when I saw it before in 1998. It remains a haunting memorial to a terrifying event that heralded the beginning of the United States' involvement in WWII.

The day was windy, wet, and cold, which made it all seem even more sinister. We moved from the Pearl Harbor memorial to a tour of the battleship USS Missouri. I had never been on a battleship before and it was huge, with thick steel walls and doors and solid everything.

The Bridge was the most impressive, many stories above the water and far from the curved front of the ship. I can't imagine how anyone could steer that enormous chunk of steel! From a distance it looks sleek and handsome, but up close, it's like a heavy peasant; bulky, solid, and unforgiving.

At the end of the tour, our guide said, "Pearl Harbor changed the world forever more. Japan did awaken the sleeping giant—the US—and nothing was the same ever again. From relationships between nations to the end of the war baby boomers, the impact of all issues related to WWII changed world cultures substantially and everlastingly."

We thawed out back at our hotel and relaxed with a beer. I had some local Kailua Pig (pulled pork) on some great purple taro bread. Taro is what they make poi out of and it is sweet and purple colored. They add some taro to the bread for color.

We strolled Waikiki beach and watched kids play and homeless people wander, and held our breath while surfers struggled or soared with the crashing waves. It was an emotional day with the contrasts of raw beauty in nature and the harsh realities of Pearl Harbor and the USS Missouri. I hurt for all the pain suffered by so many in WWII.

Rochester, Minnesota

This wasn't a vacation. We discovered in late fall 2007 that Onno was having some issues with his foot and hand that might stem from a pinched nerve in his neck. We had originally planned a cruise with some folks from my Sweet Adelines chorus and a subsequent visit to California in January, but after a scary-looking series of x-rays, doctors at the Mayo Clinic told us that it would be wise to cancel our trip. We did, and Onno had neck surgery on January 2, 2008.

He had serious bone spurs that were pressing on his spinal cord and preventing the movement of spinal fluid and causing nerve damage. The surgeon removed a one-inch wide piece from the back of three and a half vertebrae in his neck. This made a cavity so the spinal cord could be released from the compression. There was no bone grafting or hardware needed, and he continues to improve in his walking as time goes on. Onno spent about five days in the hospital and I stayed at the hotel across the street. We were glad to get home and spent the rest of the winter getting him healed up.

One odd thing was that Onno had very little pain before the surgery and everything suggested that there should be a great deal of it. We never have found out why, but we are thankful for that, and for the superb care he received at Mayo. Interestingly, I've heard that people who eat very hot food have a high tolerance for pain. Considering all of the hot peppers that Onno loves, this might be the answer.

Of course, Onno thought that he would back to playing tennis a month after the surgery, and that didn't happen. The slow recovery has been frustrating for him, but he is improving. At our last visit to the Clinic, the doctor said that there is some slight permanent paralysis from the long compression of the spinal cord, but he could regain more movement within 12-18 months after the surgery. We hope for that.

Florida

April 2008. We spent a terrific time with Hendrik and Marsha in Clearwater, Florida, after we had postponed this trip until Onno was healed enough from his surgery. We've gone to see them other times, and they in turn, spend time at what they call "The VanDemmeltraadt Bed and Breakfast," while they travel between winter in Florida and summer in Wisconsin. We always have a great time together, playing tennis and of course, eating. They have shared wonderful recipes like **Tortellini Soup, Bami Soup, Babi Ketjap,** and more.

We played tennis at a nearby clay court almost every day we were with them, and it was a great time. Marsha and I went to a liquor store for some beer one day and my heel got caught in the door. It got pretty banged up with a nasty cut and bruise, but I limped around for a few days and it healed up fine.

As pre-arranged, we picked up a rental car and drove past the Sarasota area to Edgerton, Florida, where my daughter-in-law Sara's family has a beautiful condo unit right on the Gulf. The whole Laun family was meeting there for a wedding celebration for Sara's brother Tim and his new wife Natalie, who had been married earlier in New York. The group included Lee and Sara, Sara's parents, Jon and Paula, plus several others of their family. Tim and Natalie served as our hosts and we had a great time on the beach. Seeing and playing with our grandkids Greta and Henry, was wonderful.

**21. Hendrik, Gloria, Onno, Marsha, Florida, 2008
A Celosse and a VanDemmeltraadt always win!**

On the final day of our visit, we all went on an adventure for the "real" wedding celebration. The adults had told all of the kids that we were going to the dentist. The cute thing was that the kids love going to the dentist, so they were fine with getting dressed up. Greta had been told that all of us had to wear socks to the dentist, so we complied and wore our socks.

Several cars full of people followed the leader into the small town in great anticipation. It turned out that as a big surprise, we went bowling! Everyone was assigned a lane, even the tiny kids, who had sides on their lanes. We were also assigned to teams and it was quite competitive. After bowling we had pizza, chicken wings and sodas. What a fun and unique celebration for a lovely couple, and it was such a joy for us to be included.

Amtrak to the West

October 18 to November 13, 2008. We began this ambitious trip with more than a little apprehension. Somehow in the planning the journey had gotten bigger and bigger. But, friends had said, "If you like the person you're traveling with and you have plenty of time, go for it!" So we did.

We went to the train depot in St. Paul, bought a month-long pass for each of us, and began to book our travel. The trip turned out to be a huge loop, starting from St. Paul to Chicago, then west to the Grand Canyon, north from California to Washington, and east across the plains and back to St. Paul.

It was a foggy morning with the sun struggling to peek through the haze, when we left St. Paul in coach class on the Empire Builder. When the mist lifted, the trees were brilliantly colored and the Mississippi River was calm and picturesque with patches of sunlight gleaming on the ripples.

In Chicago, we stayed overnight at the beautiful Palmer House hotel, and thoroughly enjoyed the elegant plush room and handsome surroundings. The elegance was even more appreciated as we anticipated the coming month of unknowns in eating and sleeping comforts.

Late the next day we boarded the Southern Chief in a small sleeper room (roomette) headed for the Grand Canyon in Williams, Arizona. We discovered quickly that the roomettes might be great for one person, but were a little too cozy for two.

Meals in the dining car were okay, but not fabulous, sort of like airplane meals, but we did get a limited choice of foods. Walking to the dining car was tricky, but we eventually adjusted to the rocking cars.

On this leg of the trip we met an interesting fellow who was part of a Japanese movie crew. They were making a documentary of train travel all over the world, and asked if they could film Onno and me in the Lounge car. Apparently they liked what they saw as they filmed us watching the passing scenery and commenting to each other, because later they asked if they could film us while eating dinner in the dining car. The filming crew of six men was on the final leg of their trip and seemed tired. They said that they had been working on this segment of the filming for 52 days and were eager to go home.

Train travel in Europe, and particularly Japan, is far superior to that in the US, both in basic infrastructure and in attention to passengers. We chatted with the crew about their experiences and learned that in the US passengers are last on the list in importance. First is the President, then the US mail, then freight, and lastly, passengers. During our trip there were many instances when we waited for a freight train to pass us by. Of course, the President rarely travels by train anymore, but should he decide to do it, he's got first dibs on getting where he wants to go.

Being filmed was fun and we might end up on the cutting room floor, but who knows, some day we might see ourselves on the big screen.

We got off the train the next evening in a barren spot in a deep forest and thankfully, a van was waiting to take us to the Grand Canyon Hotel in

Williams, Arizona, where we stayed for a couple of nights. We took a separate tour to the Grand Canyon via another train and a bus, and were totally awed by the grandeur of the Canyon, as anyone would be.

22. Gloria and Onno at the Grand Canyon.

After the tour we boarded the Grand Canyon Railway train, drank champagne and got "robbed" by some play-acting cowboy rustlers and went back to Williams. We ate at a dinner buffet, which was not the best, and went to bed early.

Back on the Southern Chief to Los Angeles in another roomette, but this was a short trip overnight. A good thing because we were climbing altitude and the toilets wouldn't always flush—yuk! We also had a delay of an hour or so because the train hit a cow on the tracks. Somebody had to climb under the train and reconnect the air hoses and clean up the mess. Onno joked that there was a special on steak the next day . . .

In Los Angeles we were whisked off to a welcome breakfast that was a fitting beginning to a week and a half of great times. We spent the first part in Apple Valley, California with Dick and Shirley Allen, friends from Onno's 3M days. We saw the homes of Roy Rogers and Dale Evans, and their graves, went to a terrific chili cook-off tasting event, and laughed a lot. I got a great recipe for oven baked mashed potatoes, **Potato Casserole** from a neighbor of the Allens.

The remainder of the time we spent with Onno's cousin Humphrey and his wife Doeschka. We met lots of lovely people, ate fantastic foods—mostly true Indonesian—**(Black Soup, Chicken Soto)** and played a new card game for us, called 51. Their hospitality was beyond compare and it was such a blessing to finally meet these beautiful people whom Onno has talked about.

Doeschka drove us to Fullerton, California to visit with Lois Stene, the only remaining sibling of Gene Cannon's. She is in a nursing home there and is 93 years old. She sincerely appreciated our sweet and touching visit, and so did I.

On the train again, this time the Coast Starlight. This train is a little newer and very nice, plus we had a "bedroom," the larger sleeper. It had its own small bathroom—much appreciated—and room to move around and sit comfortably. If we ever travel again by train, this is the way to go. The trip from Los Angeles to Seattle is indescribably beautiful and many people we met on this trip say that if a person plans only one train trip, this is the one to take. For a long part of the trip, we had the Pacific Ocean on one side of us, and mountains on the other. There was warmth and sunshine, as well as snow when we climbed the mountains, with breathtaking views at every turn.

We got off the train in Longview, Washington and had a good visit with Onno's brother Huibert and his wife, Judy. We were surprised and happy to also see their daughter Marge and her family, husband Wayne, and sons Sam and Matt.

Huibert then drove us to Portland, Oregon to my son Lee and Sara's house for a tearful and happy reunion with my grandchildren Greta and Henry. We celebrated Henry's third birthday with **chocolate beet cake**, and had a busy and joyful time, including a trip to the Oregon Zoo with Greta. That was good "alone time" for her with Opa and Grandma.

The last leg of the Amtrak trip was from Portland across Montana and North Dakota back to St. Paul on the Empire Builder again. We had a bedroom on this train this time, and it was comfortable. Unfortunately, the most beautiful part of this trip was at night, so we mainly saw prairie and far off mountains in hazy darkness. However, the vastness and relentless variety of the terrain of the US was remarkably moving and imposing throughout our trip, and the quiet prairies were a gentle way to bring this adventure to an end.

Chapter 8

Thanks for our blessings

23. Miki, Gloria, Diane and Toni

Onno and I are exceedingly blessed with loving friends and lasting friendships. My friends have embraced Onno, and his have embraced me, and we are both so grateful. I particularly appreciate the openness of Marjanne's close friends in accepting me so beautifully. When she knew she was dying, Marjanne asked her friends Toni and Diane to "watch over Onno," and that they did—closely. Both were keenly aware of how the relationship between Onno and me grew, and when they came to know me, also, our friendship grew.

We all love to cook and share recipes. I found a new one for a decadently delightful rum-filled cake, and made it for all of us workers to eat at Diane's garage sale. It was much enjoyed on a cold and rainy day. Diane is sharing some of her great desserts, one made with apples from their own orchard. Her husband Dave says that you have to use at least three different kinds of apples for any kind of apple recipe. He's right.

Recipes: Rum Cake
Plum Crunch
Apple Crisp
Apple Sauce

Dinner parties are a favorite form of entertainment and we travel back and forth to each other's houses for terrific food and lots of laughter. Here's a group that was gathered at my brother's house for an engagement party prior to Onno's and my wedding. It seemed to set the stage for a whole lot of eating thereafter!

24. Some dear friends; Dexter, Toni, Miki, Ron, Sharon, Don, Joan.

Our families have been sensitive and caring in accepting both of us and this new union. We now have 20 grandchildren between us, wow! Some of our children and grandchildren are in contact with each other via email and the like, and that is nice to know. The babies born since our marriage, at this point Henry in '05, and Isabella in '07, have united us even more strongly.

Having Onno's son Mark and his wife Sharon and their three daughters living right across the street from us is really fun. His daughter Jennifer and her family live nearby also, and nephew Al, but all of my children and their families are at least an hour and a half away. This makes our visits very special when we do get together.

We try to have occasional group gatherings, although there are really more people than any house can hold. We've had at least one major get-together in April 2006 at a local motel with almost everyone there—remarkable! We should have hired a photographer for the day, but of course didn't get it done. And, as might be expected, the batteries in my camera died, so we didn't get very many pictures of the event. We did have a rousing good time, and that's the best part.

We pray that these blessings continue, but we know that life is fickle. As I look back over these pages and the memories wash over me, I am grateful for all of the experiences that have influenced my life, good and not so good. Each one of us is who we are because of the people and events that touch our lives. What we do with those experiences is up to us, and to God.

May you, dear reader, be touched by my story if only to help you understand and appreciate your own wealth and depth of encounters that have helped to make you the person you have become. And, may you accept that person with gratitude and joy as I have learned to do with myself.

God's blessings to you and bon appetite!

25. The Cannon-VanDemmeltraadt families and friends, April 2006. Find them if you can (some may be missing or not yet born): Onno and Gloria, Albert, Gabriella, and Rachel; Bruce, Cassie, and Nate; Paula Q.; Greg, Lori, and Ian; Renee, Charlie, Jason D., Jessica D., Alyssa, Jason L., Bryce, Bre, Tyler, Brady, and Chas; Paul; Mark C., Sue, Jessica C., Joe, Connor, and Stephanie; Karen, Steve, Hannah, and Noah; Lee, Sara, Greta, and Henry; Mark V., Sharon, Katie, Josie, and Isabella; Jennifer, Perry, Breana, Ross, and Madison; Rob, Heather, Dakota, Tanner, and Bennett.

Recipes

Musing and Munching
A Memoir and Cookbook

MUSING AND MUNCHING RECIPES
CONTENTS

Breakfast

Baked Apple Pancakes 117
Caramel Apple Baked French Toast 117
Crepes 118
French Toast 118
Quiche 118
Omelet 119
Sausage Bake 119
Scrambled Eggs 120
Scrambled Eggs, Deluxe 120
Scrambled Eggs, Gourmet Style 120
Spinach Soufflé 121
Sticky buns 122

Appetizers

Artichoke Garlic Breadstick Dip 123
Bean Dip 123
Cheese Balls 124
Chicken Wings—Glazed 124
Guacamole 124
Jelly and Cream Cheese 125
Krupuk (Shrimp crackers) 125
Meatballs for Appetizers 125
Oyster Crackers 125
Sambal Goreng Kentang (shoestring potatoes with seasoning) ... 126
Tabouli 126
Taco Dip, Layered 127
Tofu, or Tahu 127

Main Dishes—Entrees

Babi Ketjap (pork in sweet soy sauce)	128
Bami (ramen noodle casserole)	128
BBQ Peanut Butter Chicken	129
Beef with Celery	129
Beef: Crock Pot Round Steak	130
Beef Stroganoff	130
Bubble and Squeak	130
Cabbage Casserole	131
Chicken, Fried	131
Chicken, Oven Baked	131
Chicken, Roasted	132
Chicken Divan	132
Chicken Citrus Stir fry	132
Chicken and Riesling	132
Chicken Pot Pie	133
Chicken Sate (or Pork)	134
Chicken Spinach Pasta	134
Chow Mein, Mock	134
Duck Casserole	135
Eggplant Casserole	135
Egg Sandwich	135
Fried Rice—or Indonesian Nasi Goreng	135
Ginger Chicken	136
Green Beans and Lamb	136
Ham Glaze/Baste	137
Hamburger Bake	137
Hamburger Bake-2	137
Hamburger Stroganoff	137
Hash	138
Kibby—Lebanese sort of meat loaf, plus variations	140
Macaroni and Cheese	141
Meatballs, Creamed	141
Meatballs, Russian	141
Meatballs, Waikiki	142
Meat Loaf-Basic	142
Meat Loaf-1	142
Meat Loaf-2	143
Meat Loaf-Quick	143
Meat Loaf-Spanish	143

Pizza Fondue 144
Pork Kebabs or Stir fry with Orange Dip 144
Pork Soft Tacos with Black Beans 145
Roast Pork—German style 145
Russian Vegetable Pie 145
Squab, Roasted 146
Sunday Dinner Roast 146
Sweet and Sour Pork 146
Scalloped Chicken 147
Scalloped Chicken or Turkey 147
Tofu with Sweet Soy Sauce 147
Torsk (Norwegian Codfish) 148
Turkey Quiche 148
Tuna or Chicken Casserole 148
Turtle, Oven Baked 149
Wild Rice Hot Dish 149

Soups

Bami Soup 150
Bean Soup 150
Black Soup (Rawon) 151
Broccoli Cream Soup 151
Cauliflower Cheese Soup 152
Chicken Soup 152
Chicken Wild Rice Soup—Low Fat 152
Chinese Chicken Soup (Soto) 153
Pea Soup 154
Tomato Soup 154
Tomato Soup, Dutch style 155
Tortellini Soup 155
Wild Rice Soup 156

Vegetables, Sauces, and Salads

Baked Potatoes 157
Baked Beans 157
Black Bean and Corn Salad 157
Boiled Beets with Orange Sauce 158
Broccoli 158
Brushetta 158

Cabbage/Cauliflower Salad 159
Cabbage, Irish 159
Caramel Apple Salad 159
Cauliflower, Tangy Mustard 160
Cheesy Potatoes 160
Corn Casserole 160
Corn-Cheese Bake 161
Cucumbers 161
Dill Pickles 161
Dried Parsley/chives/cilantro/mint, etc. 162
Freezing Fresh Corn 162
Gado Gado-Indonesian Salad 162
Green Bean Casserole 162
Hutspot—Dutch Potatoes and Carrots 163
Katie's Potatoes 163
Macaroni Salad 163
Mashed Potato Cakes 164
Peanut Sauce 164
Potato Casserole 164
Pumpkin 165
Ramen Noodle Salad 165
Tomatoes 166
Vegetable Hot Dish 166

Desserts

Almond Puff 167
Angel Cookies 167
Angel Food Cake Endless Possibilities 168
Apple Sauce 168
Apple Crisp 169
Bananas, Fried 169
Boter Koek (Shortbread Cookies) 169
Brownies-1 170
Brownies-2 170
Brownies-3 170
Butter Balls 171
Butter Mochi 171
Caramel Popcorn 171
Chocolate Beet Cake 172
Chocolate Cherry Bars 172

Chocolate Chip Oatmeal Bars 172
Chocolate Frosting 173
Club® Cracker Cookies 173
Fudge 173
Fattigmand 174
Granola Bars 174
Grapes 174
Key Lime Pie 174
Krumkake 175
Lemon Bars 1 175
Lemon Bars 2 175
Lemon Meringue Pie 176
Macadamia Nut Cake 176
Magic Marshmallow Puff-Ups 177
Marzipan 177
Queen Elizabeth II Cake 177
Pecans, Candied 178
Pie Crust 178
Plum Crunch 178
Pretzels with Caramels 179
Prune Kolaches 179
Rhubarb Cake 180
Rosettes 180
Rum Cake 180
Toffee Bars 181

Drinks

Fruit Slush 182
Pink Vodka Slush 182
Raspberry Punch 182

Fun Stuff: Notes, reminders, interesting stuff, and doo dads

Bread Crumbs 183
Cough Syrup 183
Olive Oil 183
Play Clay 184
Smelly Dishcloths 184
Spice Sachet 184

Breakfast

Baked Apple Pancakes

(Gloria—an old-fashioned iron skillet works best for this, but I've also used glass pie dishes, too)
¼ cup butter
2 tart apples, sliced
2 Tbsp sugar **(for apples), 2 tsp. sugar (for batter)**
½ cup flour, 2 eggs, ½ cup milk, ½ tsp. salt, a sprinkle of cinnamon

Melt butter in iron skillet. Add apples and 2 Tbsp. sugar, sauté 1 minute, set aside.

Combine remaining ingredients and whisk until smooth. Let stand 30 minutes (or instead as I do, take the eggs out of the fridge the night before so they are warm, and heat the milk very slightly). You want the batter room temperature when it goes into the oven.

Reheat apples to bubbling and pour them on the batter. Bake in the skillet at 425 until puffed up around the edges and golden, about 20 minutes. Sprinkle with powdered sugar or serve with syrup.

Caramel Apple Baked French Toast

1 1/2 cups Whipping Cream, 1 1/2 cups brown sugar
2 cups finely chopped, peeled apples, 1 teaspoon cinnamon
1 loaf soft Italian bread, cut into 1/2 inch cubes (10 cups)
6 eggs, 1 cup Milk, 1 teaspoon vanilla, 1 teaspoon salt

Combine whipping cream and brown sugar in 13x9-inch baking pan; mix until well blended. Toss apples with cinnamon to coat.

Layer half of bread cubes over whipped cream mixture. Sprinkle with apples. Top with remaining bread cubes. Press lightly into pan. Combine eggs, milk, vanilla and salt; beat well. Pour over bread cubes. Cover; refrigerate overnight.

Heat oven to 350°F. Bake uncovered about an hour or until set. Let stand 5 minutes. Serve caramel side up. Makes 8 to 10 servings.

Crepes

(Onno makes this! He learned to make these by watching Matje, his grandmother's sister and his beloved childhood nanny) (makes about 7-8 small crepes)

½ cup flour
½ tsp. salt, 1 Tbsp. sugar, 2 beaten eggs, 2/3 cup milk
1 tbsp. melted butter, ½ tsp. grated orange rind.

Mix all together with electric beater. Pour into crepe pan or frying pan. Batter should be thin, so crepes are thin. Can be made ahead and kept warm.

Variations—Add to batter: coffee extract/ coconut/ cinnamon

French Toast

(Gloria and Onno) for 2
Beat well with fork: 2 eggs, 2 Tbsp. milk, 1 tsp. vanilla, salt/pepper
Soak 4 slices grainy bread in the egg mixture. Put in hot fry pan with some oil. Pour the rest of the egg mixture over the bread. Lower heat, cover, and cook slowly for a few minutes so the egg cooks through the bread. Sprinkle cinnamon on bread while in the pan; turn as needed. Uncover, raise heat at end to brown. Serve on warm plates with crisp bacon or sausage and fruit.

Quiche

(originally came from Curves for Women in Lake Elmo but of course this has my adjustments) 6 servings; low calorie

Crust: (this is the best part—you can put most any filling in this low calorie and delicious crust)

2 Tbsp. olive oil
½ onion, thinly sliced, 1 ½ cups mushrooms (fresh or canned)
1 cup (packed hard) chopped baby spinach leaves
Salt/pepper to taste
2 Tbsp. yellow cornmeal, 2 Tbsp. water

Heat olive oil in skillet. Add onion and sauté until it begins to brown. Add mushrooms and stir and cook until they begin to brown. Add spinach, salt and pepper and cook briefly. Add cornmeal and water and stir well. Lightly coat a

9" pie plate with cooking spray. Press mixture over bottom and partway up the sides of pie plate. Set aside.

Filling:
6 eggs, ½ cup fat free half and half
¼ tsp salt/dash of pepper
6 ounces extra sharp cheddar cheese, shredded
¾ cup (3 ounces) diced ham (or cooked/drained sausage)

Beat eggs, half and half and seasonings thoroughly. Fold in cheese and meat. Pour filling into crust and bake at 350 for 40 minutes. Allow to stand at least 10 minutes before serving.

Omelet

3 eggs
1 Tbsp. water
Dash white pepper
Dash basil
1 tsp. dried parsley
Dash celery salt
Dash tarragon

Beat all with fork in a bowl.

In a fry pan, Sauté in a little olive oil: 2 small green onions, diced.

Add a handful of bacon bits or some crisp bacon pieces. Add egg mixture. Cook on medium heat. When almost done, fold over. Sprinkle with grated parmesan cheese. (other cheese can be added to omelet while cooking)

Sausage Bake

8 slices cubed bread
2 cups grated cheddar
1 onion, diced
1 red sweet pepper, diced
2 pounds precooked sausage (any kind, links or patties)
4 eggs, beaten
2 ½ cups milk
1 can cream of mushroom soup
½ cup milk

In greased 9x13 pan, layer bread, cheese, sausage. Blend eggs and milk and mix in the onion and red pepper, pour over the rest. Refrigerate overnight. Blend soup and the ½ cup of milk and pour over the dish before baking. Bake at 300 for 1 ½ hours.

Scrambled Eggs

(per daughter Karen about her husband Steve Ellefson's recipe, They are simply to die for!!)

8 Eggs, splash of milk, 3 Tbsp. sour cream, finely chopped onion, seasoned salt, oregano, cilantro, lemon pepper

Whip and scramble in a fry pan.

He does also crumble some left over bacon or sausage while cooking when we have it. Sorry—he does not know amounts, he is a dumper like many of the rest of us great cooks! Per Karen, "He also says to tell you that you are pretty special as he does not give his secrets out to many people."

Scrambled Eggs, Deluxe

(Gloria) 2 servings
2 ounces cream cheese
1 Tbsp. milk
3 eggs
½ cup diced cooked deli ham (or cooked bacon or sausage if preferred)
1 green onion with top, thinly sliced
1 tsp. butter or margarine

Microwave cream cheese and milk till soft. Add eggs, whisk till blended.

Sauté green onion in butter, add ham and then egg mixture. Cook and stir just until eggs are set. Serve immediately.

Scrambled Eggs, Gourmet Style

(Gloria) serves 6

This is basically just purchased frozen pastry shells (found in your grocery freezer section) filled with scrambled eggs, and topped with a hot cheese sauce. Easy and terrific weekend breakfast, simple to make, but elegant and really nummy!

Cheese Sauce:

2 Tbsp. butter, 1 ½ Tbsp. flour, 1 ¼ cup milk, dash salt

¾ cup shredded Swiss cheese, ½ cup shredded Parmesan cheese

Melt butter in saucepan over medium heat. Add flour and whisk until smooth; about 1 minute

Whisk in milk and salt, and whisk until mixture thickens slightly, about 1 more minute. Whisk in cheeses. Stir until mixture is smooth and begins to bubble, stirring constantly, about 2 minutes. Cover and keep warm.

Another easier sauce you can use is a can of cream of mushroom soup, a little milk or water, plus some grated white or yellow cheese.

Pastry shells:

Bake the frozen puff pastry shells as directed on package (20 minutes at 400; remove tops and scoop out and throw away the little bit of unbaked gooey pastry from inside, so you have hollow shells. Serve 1 to 2 per person (they usually come 6 to a package). When shells are almost done baking, Whisk 6-8 eggs; add ¼ cup or less milk; salt and pepper to taste.

Melt 1 Tbsp. butter in skillet; when butter foams, add the egg mixture. Stir eggs with spatula while cooking, until eggs are light and fluffy.

Fill shells with eggs; top each with 2-3 Tbsp. of cheese sauce; sprinkle with fresh chopped chives or parsley, and top with shell top.

Serve with juice and some fruit garnish for an elegant breakfast.

Spinach Soufflé

(Greg and Lori Cannon—they love to cook "Gourmet" meals and do it together, and this is a good example of their efforts)

1 can cream of chicken soup
½ cup each of shredded Jack and Swiss cheese
1 tsp. dry mustard, ¼ tsp. ground nutmeg
6 eggs
1 package frozen spinach or 10-12 ounces fresh (fresh is better)
¼ cup finely chopped green onion, with tops, 2 tsp. lemon juice

For proper effect, explain to your spouse how difficult it is to get soufflés to turn out right.

Butter a 2 quart soufflé or baking dish. Preheat oven to 375. In a large fry pan, combine soup, cheeses, mustard and nutmeg. Cook over low heat, stirring until cheese melts. Cool slightly.

Separate eggs, yolks into mixture, whites in large bowl. Add spinach, onions and lemon juice to cheese mixture.

Beat those egg whites! They should be really peaky. Fold ¼ of the whites into soup/cheese mixture, then pour mixture onto the rest of the egg whites. Now gently fold it all together just until white lumps disappear. Pour into soufflé dish and bake. Tell the teenagers next door to turn the music down for 35 minutes or until center feels firm. Serves 6. We like this for Sunday brunch with ham and fruit.

Sticky buns

(Karen Ellefson)

1 four-pack package of buttermilk biscuits (Kind of like the Hungry Jack kind in the tube—they sell them in a 4-pack)

1 cup of vanilla ice cream

1 stick of butter

1 cup of brown sugar

Open 2 of the biscuit rolls and cut each biscuit into quarters

Roll these in a mixture of brown sugar, white sugar and cinnamon—never measure, just dump and mix!

Put these into the bottom of a greased fluted round cake pan

You can get the other 2 rolls of biscuits ready in the same way but don't put in yet . . .

In a saucepan, combine the butter, sugar and ice cream and boil gently until thickened into a caramel consistency. Pour 1/2 of the mixture of the rolls in the pan and then add rest of biscuits and top with rest of the caramel.

Bake at 350 for 30 minutes and immediately flip the rolls out onto plate.

Appetizers

Artichoke Garlic Breadstick Dip

(Renee Cannon)
1 can artichoke hearts chopped fine
¾ cup grated parmesan cheese
¼ cup shredded mozzarella cheese
1 cup real mayonnaise
2 cloves crushed garlic
1 Tbsp. lemon juice
Combine all in baking dish. Sprinkle top with paprika. Bake at 350 for 20-30 minutes. Serve with 8-10 soft breadsticks.

Bean Dip

(Karen Miller)
1 green pepper; 1 red pepper; 1 med red onion; well chopped
2 cans black beans, drained and rinsed
1 can whole kernel corn, drained and rinsed
2 small cans green chilies (chopped, pre-done)
1 cup Italian dressing (any kind)
1 Tbsp. lime juice, 1 tsp, chili powder, ¾ tsp. cumin
1 tsp. chopped cilantro or parsley, fresh or dried
Mix all together, store in refrigerator; dip tortilla chips or scoops.

Cheese Balls

(Marsha Celosse) Terrific appetizer and Onno loves them!
½ pound softened butter (or half-butter and half-fake stuff if you insist)
8 oz. jar of grated parmesan cheese
2 cups flour
Mix all together well, roll in small balls. Bake at 350 for at least 15 minutes. Do not underbake. Cool and store in something like the jar from the parmesan cheese; keeps a long time if kept covered.

Chicken Wings—Glazed

(Renee Cannon)
2 pounds chicken wings (about 12) or dummies
¼ cup honey
2 Tbsp. soy sauce
2 Tbsp. vegetable oil
2 Tbsp. catsup
1 Tbsp. lemon juice
1 Tbsp. cornstarch
½ tsp garlic powder
Mix above ingredients and pour over chicken at least 1 hour before cooking. Put chicken on broiler pan (covered with foil and cleanup is easier). Baste with remaining marinade. Bake uncovered at 375 for 30 minutes, turn and baste, bake for another 30 minutes.

Guacamole

(Gabriella VanDemmeltraadt and Gloria created this together for a family gathering)
1 avocado, mashed
Finely chopped onion, about 1 Tbsp.
1 Tbsp. lemon juice, 1 Tbsp. sour cream, dash of salt
Extra virgin olive oil (1 tsp. at a time till it's right)
Mix all together and enjoy with any sort of chips

Jelly and Cream Cheese

(Toni Ziton)
Buy or make yourself a jar of *hot* pepper jelly. (Toni makes wonderful crabapple-hot pepper jelly)
Spread it on top of softened cream cheese in a pretty dish. Serve with good crisp crackers for guests to dip or spread.

Krupuk (Shrimp crackers)

(Gloria) Krupuk is a generic name for any crisp Indonesian cracker.
Buy dried krupuk at a good Asian food store. Heat deep fryer about half-full of vegetable oil (note: many Asian foods are prepared in peanut oil instead of vegetable oil, but we have nut allergies in the family and have to be careful).
Deep fry krupuk until light brown (it swells up at least triple in size). Drain well on paper towels and store tightly to keep crisp. Serve with any Asian food.
Another really good Krupuk is **Emping**, a crisp cracker that can be sweet or hot/sweet. It's made from some sort of nut or oat and has a different taste, but is also called **Krupuk** because it's a crisp cracker eaten with meals.

Meatballs for Appetizers

(Pat Urtel)
2 pounds of cooked meatballs (do yourself a favor and buy them-the frozen ones are great)
2 cans cream of mushroom soup
½ envelope dry onion soup mix
1 pint half and half
Mix together and put in crock pot for about 3 hours.

Oyster Crackers

(Shirley Rau and Carlotta Neutzling)
1 bag of oyster crackers
½ to 1 cup vegetable oil (to taste; I use ½ cup of extra virgin olive oil)
1 package dry Italian salad dressing
Dill weed and garlic powder to taste
Pour oil over crackers in a big bowl. Add dry salad dressing and seasonings. Stir until mixed well. Put it on a cookie sheet and heat in oven to toast it a little, stirring every few minutes (325 for about 30 minutes). Great with tomato soup or as an appetizer snack! (Can use a dry ranch dressing instead for a different taste.)

Sambal Goreng Kentang (shoestring potatoes with seasoning)

(Gloria/Marsha Celosse/Elly Mettler)
1 large can shoestring potatoes (industrial size like a 3 pound coffee can)
Dump potatoes in a very large bowl
In a fry pan, sauté:
2-3 Tbsp. butter or butter substitute
½ tsp. + minced garlic
Finely chopped onion (about half of a medium onion)
Gula java shavings (ask me about that . . . it's Indonesian coconut sugar) **or** dark brown sugar, about 1/3 cup
1 tsp. ground fresh chili paste—this is *hot*) **or** a dash of your favorite hot sauce
A dash of balsamic vinegar
Stir fry the stuff in the frying pan for a few minutes till bubbly.
Pour over the potatoes and stir well.
Spread in 2 cookie sheets with sides. Bake at 300 about 45 minutes to dry it out; stir a couple of times. Remove from oven and let sit till cool. Store in tight containers and it will stay crisp and nummy. Serve with bami, or fried rice, or eat as a snack.

Tabouli

(Toni Ziton) first a little history:
Tabouli, traditionally made with Bulgur wheat, fresh parsley, tomatoes and onions with a squeeze of lemon juice, is a middle eastern dish thought to have originated in Lebanon. Bulgur wheat, the basis of Tabouli, has been around for about 4,000 years. It is made from soaking or cooking wheat berries, then drying them and breaking the wheat kernel into even smaller pieces. The result is a grain product that has a hearty shelf life due to its insect and mold resistant properties.
1 cup of finely cracked/crushed wheat. Soak the wheat in water in large mixing bowl at least ½ hour. Cup the wheat in your hand and squeeze out excess water as tight as possible. Set aside.
1 bunch green onions, chopped fine
2 large bunches parsley, washed and cut fine (use a scissors)
¾ cup fresh finely chopped mint or ¼ cup dried mint
4 large tomatoes, chopped
½ cup olive oil or vegetable oil
Salt and pepper to taste
Juice of 4 lemons
Chop everything very fine and toss all together. Serve in a bowl to scoop onto little triangles of pita or other flat bread, or on fresh lettuce or grape leaves, or steamed cabbage leaves.

Taco Dip, Layered

(Renee Cannon)
1 package (8 oz) cream cheese, softened
1 16 ounce carton sour cream
1 package dry taco seasoning mix
1 onion, chopped
1 16 ounce bag shredded lettuce
2-3 fresh tomatoes, chopped
3 cups shredded cheddar cheese
2-3 14 ounce bags tortilla chips

Combine softened cream cheese, sour cream and taco seasoning, mix well. Spread in bottom of 9x12 pan. Sprinkle chopped onion, shredded lettuce, tomatoes on top of cream cheese. Cover top with cheddar. Serve with chips.

Tofu, or Tahu

(per Onno, who makes this—he now has 2 items in his cooking repertoire!)

Use 1 pound of firm or extra firm tofu. Dry with paper towels well, then slice in two from the middle. Sprinkle each half with garlic powder and salt, and cut into small pieces, about ¾ inch square. Deep fry in small batches in hot oil for about 5 minutes, until brown. Sprinkle lightly with more garlic and salt, if needed. Serve as appetizer or with any Asian meal as extra protein.

Even people who don't like tofu (like little kids) love this. It's crispy on the outside and soft on the inside and delicious!

Main Dishes—Entrees

Babi Ketjap (pork in sweet soy sauce)

(Gloria's version as revised from many Indo folks)
1 pound lean pork, cut in small cubes
Salt and pepper
1 onion, chopped
1 clove garlic, minced
2 Tbsp. oil
½ tsp. ginger (or more if you like)
½ to 1 tsp. sambal (chili paste or a little Tabasco)
½ cup ketjap manis (sweet soy sauce)
A dash of white vinegar

Slowly brown meat in oil with a little salt and pepper on it. Add onion and garlic and other seasonings. Add about ½ cup water to simmer meat in (about 30 minutes)
Serve on rice.

Bami (ramen noodle casserole)

(Marjanne VanDemmeltraadt, with Gloria's additions) serves 6+ people
4 packages oriental flavor ramen noodle soup mix, (save spice packs, break up noodles; I put them in a plastic bag and hit with the rolling pin a few times to break up)
2 bunches green onions or 1 leek, diced
3 cups shredded cabbage (regular green cabbage or Napa cabbage, or both)
3 ribs of celery, diced

Other green vegetables; pea pods, fresh green beans, zucchini, bok choy (no carrots or vegetables that are not green)
1 ½ cups diced cooked meat (pork, ham, chicken, shrimp, or a combination)
1 small package bean sprouts

Boil noodles (barely 3 minutes) drain and rinse; put noodles back into the big pot and add spice packets and the meat. In some olive oil in a frying pan, sauté all vegetables briefly. Add to the noodles pot and heat. Stir in bean sprouts last. Serve right away so vegetables are still crisp, although it's good to take to a pot luck and always goes fast.

BBQ Peanut Butter Chicken

1 cup peanut butter
¼ cup soy sauce
¼ cup white wine vinegar
¼ cup lemon juice
6 cloves chopped garlic
2 tsp. chopped ginger
(optional: 1 tsp. red pepper flakes)
2 ½ pounds chicken breast cut in strips

Prepare marinade and add water if needed. Marinate chicken for at least 2 hours. Grill on oiled tinfoil on the grill, or cook in a non-stick fry pan.

Beef with Celery

½ pound lean beef, thinly sliced. Put in a bowl and stir in 1 Tbsp. cornstarch and 1 Tbsp. low-salt soy sauce. Set aside.
2 cups sliced celery
3 Tbsp. oil (I use light olive oil for frying)
1/3 cup water or soup stock (to make a quick soup stock, add 1 chicken bouillon cube to a scant cup of water and microwave)
2 ounce can mushroom pieces

Heat oil in wok or deep fry pan. Stir-fry beef until browned. Remove and add celery to the pan. Toss briefly, pour in water or soup stock, and mushrooms, cover. After 4 minutes, return beef to pan. Heat with cover off. Serve at once.

This recipe works well with broccoli instead of celery. I also add onion and if I have them, use fresh mushrooms.

Beef: Crock Pot Round Steak

(Shirley Allen)
Round steak for 4 (about 1+ pound); cut in 3 inch cubes.
Coat in flour and put in crock pot/slow cooker. Add 1 cup water and 1 package dry onion soup mix, some garlic powder and pepper (no salt). Cook on low for 8 hours.
Serve over mashed potatoes.

Beef Stroganoff

1 ½ pounds beef (round steak or other steak on the tender side) Cut into ¼ inch slices and sauté in large frying pan in butter for about 2 minutes. Remove and set aside.
Sauté:
1 bunch green onions, cut small
¾ pound cut fresh mushrooms
Add the cooked beef and season with salt and pepper, a dash of nutmeg and ½ tsp. basil. A little parsley is good, too.
Add and heat, but do not boil: ¼ cup white wine (or ¼ cup beef bouillon) and 1 cup sour cream.
Serve over green noodles or rice.

Bubble and Squeak

(from England via Daphne Brackley. Daphne says that this was used in war time—WWII—for leftover vegetables; basically cabbage and potatoes. You just mixed it all together and fried it crisp like a large patty.)
1/2 medium head cabbage, sliced up thin
3 slices bacon, diced (or precooked bacon bits)
1 onion, chopped
1 cup cubed cooked ham (if desired)
1 tablespoon butter
3 cups cooked potatoes—thinly sliced, or use mashed potatoes, fresh or left over
1/2 teaspoon paprika, salt and pepper to taste
In a medium saucepan, cook cabbage in a small amount of water for about 5 minutes, or until tender. Drain, and set aside.
In a skillet (a cast iron skillet works best) cook bacon and onion until onion is soft and bacon is crisp. Add ham, and cook until heated through. Add butter,

then mix in the cooked cabbage and potatoes. Season with paprika, salt, and pepper. Cook until browned on bottom, turn, and brown again.

Cabbage Casserole

(Shirley Rau)
Sauté in large fry pan:
1 medium chopped onion, 3 Tbsp. butter
Add ½ pound ground beef—not too browned, ½ tsp. salt and dash of pepper
In casserole dish, put in 3 cups coarsely shredded cabbage.
Cover the cabbage with the meat mixture
Top with 3 more cups of cabbage.
Pour 1 can tomato soup over the top. Bake, covered for 1 hour at 350

Chicken, Fried

1 chicken, cut in pieces (or just buy one all cut up)
Wash pieces and pat dry with paper towel.
Dip pieces in a little milk in a bowl.
Dredge in a dish with some parmesan cheese mixed with some flour, salt and pepper, plus a couple of teaspoons of Italian seasoned dry bread crumbs.
Brown in hot oil for a few minutes, cover and turn heat down until done—you can add a little water (15 minutes or so). Remove cover and cook till desired brownness.

Chicken, Oven Baked

(tongue in cheek, Gloria to Allene Moesler for her bridal shower recipe in 1964. I can't believe I did this, but I guess that was the extent of my cooking in those days!)
Preheat oven to 375
Remove TV dinner from carton
Place in oven
Wait 25 minutes
Open oven
Grasp tray—ouch!—use pot holders—stupid!
Place on table
Eat
Easy wasn't it!

Chicken, Roasted

(Gloria, from farm years)
1 whole fat chicken (or a duck or other fowl)
Put in roaster pan and sprinkle with 1 package dry onion soup mix. Add a little water, cover the roaster and bake at 350 for about 2 hours.

For wild meat, bake at a lower temperature for longer. The onion soup takes the wild taste away.

Chicken Divan

(Betty D. no clue who this is . . . recipe is in Karen's young girl writing)
(have the same recipe from Shirley Rau without the curry)
2 10 oz pkgs. frozen broccoli spears
2 cups or 3 breasts of cooked chicken
2 cans cream of chicken soup
1 cup mayonnaise
1 tsp. lemon juice, ½ tsp. curry powder
½ cup shredded cheddar cheese, or ¼ cup cheddar & ¼ cup American

Cook broccoli and arrange in 9x13 greased pan. Put chicken on top. Combine soup, mayo and seasonings, and pour over chicken. Sprinkle cheese on top.

Toss ½ cup soft bread cubes in 1 Tbsp. melted butter, sprinkle over the top of all. Bake at 350 for 30 minutes.

Chicken Citrus Stir fry

(Marsha Celosse's friend)
Whisk together:
½ cup orange juice, ¼ cup teriyaki sauce, 2 tsp. soy sauce, 2 tsp. cornstarch
Stir fry:
1 Tbsp. canola oil
1 pound chicken breasts, cut up, 1 red pepper sliced, ½ pound snow peas
Fry meat first, then add vegetables, then sauce. Serve on rice.

Chicken and Riesling

(Greg and Lori Cannon, Gourmet at its highest) serves 4
4 boned chicken breasts (note: turkey works well, and shrimp is a killer)
3 Tbsp. butter, 1 Tbsp. oil

2 Tbsp. minced green onions
¼ cup brandy
¼ pound sliced mushrooms
1 ½ cups good white wine
½ cup heavy cream
1 Tbsp. corn starch
Cooked wide noodles, fettuccini, or rice

Sprinkle the boned chicken breasts lightly with salt and white pepper. In a large skillet, sauté the chicken pieces in the butter and oil for 2-3 minutes on each side. Add the onions and cook with the chicken for another 2 minutes. Heat the brandy in a separate pan and pour it over the chicken. Flame it and shake the skillet until the flames die out. Add the mushrooms and wine and cover the skillet. Cook the chicken over low heat for about 20 minutes. Transfer the chicken to a warmed serving platter. Skim off any fat from the pan juices. Mix the cornstarch into the heavy cream and add this to the pan juices. Cook, stirring, until thickened and smooth. Add salt and white pepper to taste. Place chicken pieces on beds of noodles or rice, and cover with sauce. Take a picture and send it to us. Pour the rest of the white wine into glasses and serve with the meal.

Chicken Pot Pie

Buy frozen pastry shells and bake as many as you need as directed on the package.

Dice and set aside:

Celery, 2 ribs, 1 carrot, 3-4 green onions, ½ red or white onion

1 cup of frozen peas or peapods/asparagus/zucchini/green beans . . . . anything goes in this recipe

Stir fry the vegetables in a little olive oil (light) for only 2-3 minutes. Add about 1 Tbsp. soy sauce.

Do not overcook the vegetables; they should be crisp when served.

Add 2 cups cut up cooked chicken (left over roasted chicken is great) and heat through.

Add 1 can cream of mushroom soup, and ¾ can milk.

1 Tbsp. cut up parsley.

Heat, but do not overcook.

At the end, toss in some bean sprouts if you like.

Serve over pastry or in pastry shells. Serves about 4. (Good over toast or rice, too.)

Chicken Sate (or Pork)

(Elly Mettler)
Chicken or pork cut in small cubes
4 Tbsp. sweet soy sauce (ketjap manis)
½ tsp. onion powder, ½ tsp. garlic powder (or minced garlic)
½ tsp. ginger, ½ tsp. curry powder, 1 tbsp. lemon juice
Mix all well and let marinate for at least 30 minutes (or overnight).
Put meat on skewers (if wooden skewers, soak in water for 15 minutes.)
Add 3 Tbsp. oil to leftover marinade and brush on sates.
Grill on barbeque for 6-8 minutes.
Serve with peanut sauce.
Note from Gloria: When I don't want to do the work of putting the meat on skewers, I just stir-fry it in a frying pan on the stove. Tastes great and it's much less work.

Chicken Spinach Pasta

For 2+ people, use ½ package basil fettuccini, cooked separately till al dente (3 minutes) drain, rinse (not overdone)
1 small chicken breast, cut in tiny pieces, 3 pieces bacon, cut small
1 cup chicken broth, salt and pepper to taste
1 package fresh spinach, 2 cloves chopped garlic, ½ chopped onion
In hot skillet, cook chicken and bacon till brown; add onion & garlic and cook till done. Add broth, seasonings and spinach; cook till spinach wilts.
Sprinkle with parsley.
Add fettuccini to meat mixture. Serve on hot plates, sprinkle with parmesan cheese.

Chow Mein, Mock

Sauté together:
1 pound hamburger, 5 sticks chopped celery, 3 Tbsp. chopped onion, or a bunch of green onions, chopped
1 can chop suey vegetables, drained
Add:
¾ cup uncooked rice, 1 can cream of mushroom soup, with 2 cans water
¼ cup soy sauce
Boil 5 minutes. Put in greased pan, bake at 350 for 1 hour.

Duck Casserole

Meat from 4 small ducks, or 1 or 2 larger ones (roasted 2 hours)
Cook in rice cooker:
2 cups white rice. 1 cup wild rice + little bit of brown rice
Mix together:
1 can sliced mushrooms, 1 large onion, diced
¼ cup soy sauce, 1 can mushroom soup, 1 can cream of chicken soup
Some water, Salt, pepper, garlic powder
Add the cooked rice and duck meat
Mix all together and put in greased large casserole. Bake 1 hour at 350. Put slivered almonds on top last 10 minutes.

Eggplant Casserole

(Gloria from a brief stint of growing eggplant on the farm)
2 medium eggplants—peeled and sliced
1 can (15 ounces) tomatoes
½ tsp. sugar, 2 cloves chopped garlic, grated parmesan cheese

Briefly cook tomatoes, sugar and garlic, covered. Fry eggplant in oil until slightly browned. Drain well on paper towels. Place layer of eggplant in casserole dish; spoon part of tomato mixture over it; sprinkle with parmesan cheese. Continue until all ingredients are used. Top with parmesan cheese. Bake at 350 for 20-30 minutes until casserole is bubbly. Serves 4.

Egg Sandwich

(Greg Cannon)
Fry one egg slowly in a fry pan. Break the yolk. Add salt and pepper and top with a good slice of Swiss cheese and cover so it melts.
Serve on bread or toast.

Fried Rice—or Indonesian Nasi Goreng

(Gloria's version) My kids loved this when they were small and I rarely made it because we didn't eat much rice when they were little—how life has changed! Of course I never heard of bok choy or other oriental vegetables then, and have become much more adventuresome when making it these days.

Bacon pieces, browned and crisp

Chopped onion, plus any leftover vegetables you have; a few snow peas, green beans, bok choy, anything goes, plus some meat (cooked chicken, beef, pork, shrimp, whatever you have)

Add a glop of soy sauce and a little oyster sauce if you have it, and you can add ¼ tsp of sambal (ground fresh chili paste) or a little crushed red pepper if you're brave.

Brown this stuff a little, then add left over rice (or fresh) about 2—3 cups cooked. Heat rice through. Add 1 well beaten egg and stir through mixture. When the egg is cooked, the rice is hot enough. Add some clipped parsley or cilantro at the end.

Onno likes a separate small omelet made of another beaten egg; cook this in a small fry pan, then slice in thin strips and put on top of the finished fried rice.

Ginger Chicken

(Gloria) I have no clue where I got this recipe, but it is really good!
2 chicken breasts, sliced thin
Sauté in Wok till golden
Add ¼ pound mushrooms and a medium onion, sliced
2 sliced carrots
1 can chicken broth
2 Tbsp. soy sauce
1 tsp. ginger root and ½ tsp. ground ginger (OR, I use about 1 ½ tsp. crushed fresh ginger that I buy in a jar and it keeps in the refrigerator for a long time)
Salt and pepper to taste
Cover and simmer 15 minutes.

Add sauce of 2 Tbsp. cornstarch in ¼ cup sherry (or chicken broth). Cook till thick.

For some color, sprinkle with fresh or dried parsley at the end. Serve over rice.

Green Beans and Lamb

(Lebanese or Syrian Loobia Bi Laham—from Toni Ziton)
1 1/2 pounds green beans (or 2 cans); wash & break beans or cut.

Brown 1 pound lamb meat cut in cubes with 2 cloves garlic until done. Add beans to meat plus 2 small cans tomato sauce & 2 cans water, salt and pepper to taste, 1 tsp. cinnamon, and simmer until beans are done, about 1 hour; makes 5 or 6 servings.

Serve with rice or rice with vermicelli.

Ham Glaze/Baste

(Renee Cannon)
1 cup yellow mustard
1 cup brown sugar
2-3 tsp. garlic
Mix together and spread on ham before/while baking.

Hamburger Bake

(Myrna Otte, from 1966 when I made my first car trip to "the cities" with Paul and Mark to see Ottes when they lived on the University campus. She says her family still asks her to make this.)
Mix together in 9x9 pan, ungreased:
1/3 cup milk or cream & 1 pound lean ground beef (add onions if wanted). Season to taste. Spread out evenly in pan.
Spread 1 can cream of chicken soup over meat (undiluted)
Bake 30 minutes at 350.
Remove from oven; arrange over top 2 cups canned shoestring potatoes.
Heat again 5-10 minutes.
(Also good with tomato soup instead of chicken)

Hamburger Bake-2

(Gloria, from early farm days)
1 pound ground beef, ½ package onion soup mix
1 package frozen mixed vegetables or 1 can drained vegetables (my kids liked corn)
1 can cream of mushroom soup, ½ can water, 1 tsp. snipped parsley
1 pound frozen round potato pieces
Brown the ground beef (add some chopped onion to the beef if wanted) and put ½ of it in the bottom of a glass casserole. Sprinkle with the onion soup mix. Put the vegetables on top of that. Add the rest of the beef. Mix the mushroom soup and water, and pour over the casserole. Top with the potato pieces. Bake at 350 for 30 minutes.

Hamburger Stroganoff

(Renee Cannon) (I had written GOOD on this recipe)
In large skillet, stir fry in ¼ cup butter:
1 pound ground beef, and 1 onion, chopped (1/2 cup) till tender.

Stir in: 2 Tbsp. flour, 1 tsp. salt, ¼ tsp. pepper, 1 clove minced garlic
1 can mushroom pieces, drained, cook and stir for 5 minutes.
Stir in 1 can cream of chicken soup; simmer uncovered for 10 minutes.
Stir in 1 cup sour cream, heat through.
Serve over 2 cups hot cooked noodles, sprinkle with snipped parsley

Hash

(Gene Cannon) makes about 25 pounds, as served at the bi-annual Cannon family reunion picnic, 7/3/1994

15 pounds choice lean beef pot roast (use 3 5# roasts, about 2-3 inches thick

8 pounds potatoes (dry white potatoes preferred, not fresh—too much moisture makes for sloppy hash)

3 pounds carrots, 6 pounds white onions, 3 pounds butter, 3 pounds marble jack cheese (Wisconsin preferred) seasoning to taste: salt, pepper, parsley or a seasoning mixture

At least 2 1.5 liter bottles of a good Liebfraumilch (German white wine)

Preparation:

Open bottle of wine; leave the cap off for 15 minutes to let gasses escape. Pour glass of wine, drink while roast is cooking.

Pot roast needs to be precooked in a large roaster 24 hours before final preparation. Roast, covered, about 45 minutes at 350; turn over midway to cook evenly. Meat should be pink in the middle. Leave covered, let set overnight in a very cool place.

Next day:

Potatoes: pour glass of wine, drink while peeling potatoes. Cut peeled potatoes into long strips, cover with slightly salted water, leave in cool place.

Carrots: pour glass of wine, sip same while peeling carrots. Cut carrots into long strips, put in water or plastic bag and keep cool until ready to grind.

Beef: skim the solidified fat off the meat and discard. Remove meat and place on cutting board. Pour the natural juice remaining in roaster into a fruit jar to use later. Slice meat into strips about ½ inch square and 3-4 inches long.

Set aside. Pour glass of wine for reserve purposes—it's going to be a long day . . .

Now prepare the onions. Start with peeling, and drink wine generously at this point. It cuts down the dripping from your eyes (that would make the hash too salty). Cut onions into quarters, set aside.

Pour another glass of wine and set up the old hand operated food grinder. Use the coarse grinding ring so the material when ground will be chunky. Now I might add that I have tried every kind of grinder, chopper, food processor, etc. known to mankind, and nothing works as well as the old fashioned hand grinder.

Take a sip of wine to restore energy level.

Begin grinding into a small container (like a flat cake pan). Grind a little beef, a little potato, a little onion, and a little carrot in equal portions so it gets really mixed well. As the small pan gets full pour it into a larger roaster. A big electric roaster works great for the final step, but you could use a big oven roaster, too.

This may take an hour or two so several sips of wine are permissible to prevent dehydration.

When finished grinding quickly wash and clean the kitchen floor before the wife comes home (a dog works for this step, also).

A good nap can be inserted here—to get ready for the next step.

Now dig out the old iron skillets. I usually use 2 12 inchers. Heat pans and begin pan-frying hash mixture in skillets using butter to keep from sticking. Fry until parts become brown and crispy here and there. Add seasoning to each batch as it fries. Don't overcook—it still has to roast later.

As each batch is fried put into roaster and start another frypan-full. This takes about 2 hours and is worth about 2 more glasses of wine. As you pour each pan full into the roaster, add whatever extra seasonings you like. When frying operation is completed you will have a roaster full of about 25 pounds of hash ready to roast. You will also be very relaxed.

Now remember earlier we saved the natural juice from the meat. Gently mix this juice (about a cupful) into the hash by stirring with a big spoon. Don't overdo it and make it mushy, but it adds good flavor. Caution: good hash stands by itself—it should not be soupy.

Now have another glass of wine as your reward for a good job in process.

At the end of one hour add 3 pounds of cheese sliced thin. Distribute through the hash sort of in layers. Then roast another half-hour or so. The cheese will disappear as it melts into the rest of the hash and taste great.

Set the roaster on warm and wait for your guests to arrive. They can be 2 or 3 hours late and it won't hurt the hash. Have another glass of wine and an additional nap if necessary.

Serve with a vegetable salad and garlic bread and enjoy!

(Be sure to dispose of the empty wine bottles before the wife comes home)

Kibby—Lebanese sort of meat loaf, plus variations

(from Toni Ziton; it's good, but it's only close to Dexter's real recipe; I can't get that and neither can anybody else)
2 pounds finely ground leg of lamb
1 ½ cups extra fine cracked wheat (burghul)
1 small onion, grated fine; salt and pepper to taste

Wash wheat good and soak in cold water for about 10 minutes. Squeeze handsful of wheat to remove most of the water and put this wheat into a large bowl. Add the meat, onion, salt and pepper. Mix and knead this mixture until it is thoroughly mixed and smooth. Dip your hands into cold water as you mix this for a better consistency.

This can be chilled and served raw as an appetizer (yuk!) (garnish with parsley and raw onion quarters, or prepared in the following ways:

Baked Kibby

Butter a 9x11 pan and spread ½ of the meat mixture over the bottom. Sprinkle with Hushwee (recipe follows) pine nuts or walnuts. Make top layer of remaining meat. Smooth top with your wet hands and cut into diamond shapes before baking. Pour 1 cup clarified butter or melted butter over the top. Bake at 325 for 50 minutes or so until the meat reaches desired doneness.

Hushwee (filling for Kibby)
½ pound coarsely ground lamb
1 medium onion finely chopped
½ cup pine nuts
1 Tbsp. butter, ½ tsp. Allspice®, ½ tsp. salt

Sauté meat in butter. When partially browned, add onions and seasonings, and pine nuts. Simmer until onions are soft; cool. Spread this mixture evenly over the bottom layer of Kibby that you've already spread in a 9x11 buttered pan. Put the top layer of Kibby over this mixture, pour melted butter over the top and bake at 325 for about 50 minutes.

Fried Kibby

Form raw Kibby mixture into patties and fry slowly in hot oil.

Raahs Kibby (hollowed balls)

Take an amount of raw Kibby about the size of an egg. Hold it in one hand and poke finger into center. Rotate the meat around your finger, enlarging the inside hollow by pressing the meat to the outside shell. When the outer shell is as thin as possible, fill with 1 tsp. Hushwee or pine nuts. Close end. At this point, the stuffed meat may be deep fried in hot oil, turning as they brown. Remove carefully and place on paper towels to drain.

Macaroni and Cheese

(Hendrik Celosse's version and close to Gloria's)
3 cups elbow macaroni, cooked and rinsed
1 ½ cup milk (Yes, you can use goat's milk if you like . . .)
Salt and pepper to taste, and nutmeg if you like it
6-8 ounces sharp cheddar cheese, grated
2 beaten eggs
2 tsp. butter
Put all in buttered casserole, top with bread crumbs (you can use Dutch bread rusks) dot with butter
Bake at 350 till done, about an hour

Meatballs, Creamed

(Renee Cannon)
1 can cream of mushroom soup, diluted with ½ cup water
1 pound ground beef
¼ cup breadcrumbs, 2 Tbsp. minced onion, 1 Tbsp. crushed parsley, 1 beaten egg
Mix ¼ cup of diluted soup mixture with remaining ingredients. Make 16 meatballs; brown in oil in skillet; pour off fat. Add rest of soup. Cover and simmer for 15 minutes; stir often. 4 servings.

Meatballs, Russian

(Renee Cannon. Renee thinks that some of these meatball recipes came from our years of ethnic dinners when we dressed in togas or turbans and spoke in tongues.)
1 ½ pound ground beef
1 12 oz. bottle of catsup
1 12 oz. bottle/can of beer
Shape beef into small meatballs; freeze. Place meatballs, catsup and beer into covered frying pan; simmer for 20 minutes. Serve as appetizers, or simmer till sauce thickens and serve with spaghetti or macaroni.

Meatballs, Waikiki

(Renee Cannon)
½ pound ground beef, 1/3 cup minced onion
1 ½ tsp. salt, ¼ tsp. ginger
¼ cup milk, 2 Tbsp. cornstarch
½ cup packed brown sugar, 1 Tbsp. soy sauce
2/3 cup cracker crumbs, 1 egg, 1 Tbsp. oil
1 can (13 ½ oz.) drained pineapple tidbits (save syrup)
1/3 cup vinegar, 1/3 cup chopped green pepper

Mix thoroughly, the beef, crumbs, onion, egg, salt, ginger and milk. Shape into balls by rounded tbsp. Brown in oil and cook till done. Remove from pan and keep warm. Drain fat from skillet.

Mix cornstarch and sugar; stir in pineapple syrup, vinegar and soy sauce till smooth. Pour into skillet; cook till thick. Boil 1 minute. Add meatballs, pineapple tidbits and green pepper, heat through.

Meat Loaf-Basic

2 cups fine bread crumbs (or oatmeal)
2/3 cup finely chopped onion
2 tsp. salt, ¼ tsp. pepper
½ cup milk
2 eggs
1 pound lean ground beef
½ pound ground pork
½ pound ground veal

This recipe can be done with any variation of ground meats as above, just use 2 pounds. Also a variation of liquids; catsup, chili sauce, tomato juice, milk, water, etc.; use enough liquid to make it all hold together but not be too soupy.

Mix all together and pat into any shape pan, and bake at 350 until done.

Meat Loaf-1

1 envelope dried onion or mushroom flavor soup mix
2 pounds ground beef
1 ½ cups bread crumbs
2 eggs

¾ cup water
½ cup catsup

In large bowl, combine all ingredients. Pack into 5 cup ring mold and invert onto jelly-roll pan (or shape into loaf in shallow baking pan). Bake 1 hour or until done at 350. Makes 6-8 servings.

Meat Loaf-2

2 pounds ground beef, lean
1 pound ground lamb
½ pound ground pork
1 chopped onion
3 eggs
¾ cup oatmeal
Salt/pepper/soy sauce/hot sauce to taste

Mix all together, put in pan, top with 3 slices of bacon. Bake at 350 for 1 ½ hours.

Meat Loaf-Quick

(Renee Cannon)

1 envelope dried onion soup mix (smack the packet with a rolling pin before opening so that onion particles are fine)
½ cup nonfat dry milk
1 cup tomato juice
2 pounds ground beef

Combine soup, milk, and tomato juice; let sit for 15 minutes. Add to beef; form into loaf. Bake 45-60 minutes at 350.

Meat Loaf-Spanish

(Renee Cannon)
1 ½ pounds ground beef
1 can (8 oz.) tomato sauce
8 large pimento-stuffed olives, sliced
1 med. onion, chopped (1/2 cup)
1/3 cups oatmeal
1 egg, salt/pepper to taste

Mix all (save 2/3 of the tomato sauce). Spread in ungreased loaf pan 9x5x3. Spread remaining tomato sauce over the loaf. Bake at 350 for 75 minutes.

Pizza Fondue

1 medium onion, chopped
½ pound ground beef
2 cans pizza sauce (10 ½ oz.)
1 Tbsp. cornstarch
1 ½ tsp. fennel seed
1 ½ tsp. oregano
¼ tsp. garlic powder
10 ounces grated cheddar cheese
1 cup grated mozzarella cheese

Brown meat and onion, mix in cornstarch and seasonings and pizza sauce. Reduce heat and stir well. When thick and bubbles, add cheese by thirds, stirring well. With fondue forks or sticks, dunk garlic bread cubes, toasted English muffins, or French bread cubes into fondue, and enjoy.

Pork Kebabs or Stir fry with Orange Dip

(Gloria) serves about 4; this is really good and very different tasting!
Cooking spray or light olive oil for frying
1 cup light sour cream
¼ cup orange marmalade
1 Tbsp. low salt soy sauce
2 tsp. sesame oil, 1 tsp. garlic, 1 tsp. ginger
1+ pounds pork tenderloins, cut into small cubes
1 large red (or orange or yellow) bell pepper, seeded & cut into cubes
Onion—cut into quarters
Salt/pepper to taste, if wanted (I don't think it needs any)

Whisk together sour cream, marmalade, soy sauce, sesame oil, garlic and ginger. Reserve ½ cup of mixture for dipping while eating.

You can either put meat, bell pepper and onion on skewers and grill, or stir fry on the stove (easier). Brush meat and veggies with sauce before and during cooking.

When stir frying, do the meat first with some of the sauce. It browns really great. When meat is done, add veggies and barely cook with a little more sauce. Serve some sauce for dipping while eating.

If you use wooden skewers, soak for 20 minutes in water before putting stuff on them so they don't scorch when you grill.

(Onno suggests adding pineapple to this, and he likes this dish better than sweet and sour pork.)

Pork Soft Tacos with Black Beans

1 Tbsp. olive oil
2 cloves minced garlic
Cooked pork cubes (can be leftover meat)
15 oz. can black beans, rinsed and drained
8 oz. can tomato sauce
1 Tbsp. minced chipotle chilies in adobo sauce
1 tsp. dried oregano
Heat the olive oil in a skillet and add all of the above. Cook slowly for about 5 minutes. Serve on warmed tortillas and add the toppings you like.
8 small flour tortillas
Toppings; shredded cheese, sour cream, shredded lettuce, diced tomatoes, sliced avocado.

Roast Pork—German style

This is the famous roast pork that is served at the annual Lake Elmo Christ Lutheran Church pork and sauerkraut supper.

Buy one large fresh pork roast. Sprinkle it liberally with Lawry's seasoned salt (® Lawry's Foods LLC) and cut a large onion in quarters and put on top. Add a little water. Roast in an electric roaster or a slow to medium oven for several hours (maybe 6-8 hours) depending on weight of roast (use a meat thermometer) then pull meat apart.

Russian Vegetable Pie

(Marjanne VanDemmeltraadt) serves 4; serve with a salad
Use ready-made deep dish pie crust (top and bottom)
On bottom crust, spread ½ package of cream cheese
Boil 5-6 eggs hard; slice and layer on cream cheese
Sauté ½ pound mushrooms, 1 bunch cut up green onion, and layer on top of eggs.
Shred cabbage and sauté with salt, tarragon, and butter until soft.
Layer cabbage on top of pie.
Put on the top crust and bake at 350 for about an hour.

Squab, Roasted

(Gloria from the farm)

The recipe is simply to wash the dressed squab, place in a baking pan, season, and roast. I sprinkled them lightly with dry onion soup mix, and baked about 60-90 minutes at 325. One bird serves a person, like a Cornish hen. They were moist and delicious, and really special, but only one time did we have an abundance of young birds to use them for a meal.

Sunday Dinner Roast

1 beef roast
1 package dry onion soup mix
1 can cream of mushroom soup
1 large piece of aluminum foil

Place roast on piece of aluminum foil large enough to wrap meat tightly. Sprinkle roast with onion soup mix. Spoon cream of mushroom soup on top of roast. Wrap tightly and place in roasting pan. Roast at 300 for 4 hours.

Variations:

This recipe works well for wild meat (old chicken, old or wild duck, wild meats like venison, rabbit) You don't have to wrap it in foil. A covered pan works well, too. You can also roast at higher temps a shorter time, but long slow cooking makes tough meat more tender.

Sweet and Sour Pork

Brown in light olive oil: 1 ½ pounds lean pork, cut in small pieces. Add ½ cup water, cover and simmer till tender.

Drain 1 can of pineapple chunks and set fruit aside.

Mix pineapple juice (it's about ½ cup) with:

¼ cup brown sugar
2 Tbsp. cornstarch
¼ cup vinegar
2-3 Tbsp. low salt soy sauce

In a separate fry pan, briefly sauté in a little olive oil (very briefly, you don't want to overcook vegetables):

1 green pepper, sliced
½ red or orange pepper, sliced
1 sliced red onion
(You can add a sliced carrot if desired)

Add meat and sauce to the vegetables; cook briefly and stir till hot and thick. Serve over rice.

Scalloped Chicken

(Gloria—good way to use leftover chicken and rice. Makes a good sized dish, cut in half for smaller version.)
3 Tbsp. butter, 2 Tbsp. flour, 2 cups chicken broth
1 cup milk, salt and pepper
3 cups cooked rice
3 cups cooked diced chicken
2 cups sliced sautéed mushrooms
½ cup slivered almonds
Buttered bread crumbs

Melt butter over low heat in a medium saucepan; stir in flour, blending well. Add chicken broth, milk, salt and pepper. Cook, stirring constantly, until thickened. Butter a 2-quart baking dish. Spread half of the rice in the bottom of the baking dish; top with half of the chicken, half of the sliced mushrooms, half of the slivered almonds. Pour in half of the sauce. Repeat layers; sprinkle with buttered bread crumbs. Bake at 350 for 45 minutes.

Scalloped Chicken or Turkey

(Grandma Vi Johnson)
1 quart cooked chicken or turkey
1 quart broth (can use canned chicken broth or juice from the meat)
1 ½ quart bread crumbs
¾ cup melted butter
½ tsp pepper, ½ tsp salt, 1 ½ tsp sage, 2 T. chopped onion

Layer chicken and dry bread crumbs. Make gravy out of broth (add a little flour to the broth). Pour over all and bake at 350 until brown—at least 45 minutes.

Tofu with Sweet Soy Sauce

(Elly Mettler—a favorite of Onno's)
Sauté 1 chopped onion, 2 cloves garlic in 2 Tbsp. oil

Add 1 tsp. Sambal Oelek (USS018-21) ground fresh chili paste, and sauté a minute more.

Add 1 cup water, 8 Tbsp. ketjap manis (sweet soy sauce) & 2 tsp. lemon juice, and bring to a soft boil.

Mix 2 tsp. corn starch with a little water. Add a little at a time to sauce until smooth and thickened. Serve with deep fried tofu and fresh bean sprouts.

Torsk (Norwegian Codfish)

(Gloria) (Oboy, Renee will remember the Torsk story from when we were all worried about the starving children in Biafra)
1 pound of cod or torsk
½ cup melted butter, ¼ cup cut up parsley, ¼ cup chopped onion, 4 oz. drained mushrooms, salt and pepper
Cut torsk into serving sized pieces and place in shallow pan. Pour remaining ingredients over the fish. Bake at 350 for 15 minutes covered, and another 15 minutes uncovered.

Turkey Quiche

(Gloria) Very old recipe—many splotches and stains on it.
1 pkg. frozen chopped broccoli, 2 cups cooked turkey, cubed,
1 cup Swiss cheese, diced, 1 small onion, diced
1 9-inch pastry shell, baked
3 eggs
1 cup heavy cream
2 Tbsp. lemon juice, salt and pepper to taste
Sprinkle broccoli, onions, turkey and cheese evenly in shell. Beat eggs, cream, lemon juice, salt and pepper until mixed but not frothy. Pour into shell. Bake in preheated oven at 375 for 35-40 minutes or until center is set. Garnish with parsley or cilantro and onion.

Tuna or Chicken Casserole

(Gloria—from early days) 4 servings
1 can cream of vegetable soup, ½ cup milk
2 cups cooked noodles
1 can (7 oz.) tuna, drained and flaked
2 Tbsp. buttered bread crumbs
1 can peas and carrots, drained (or frozen)
Blend soup and milk. Add noodles, tuna, peas and carrots. Pour into 1 ½ qt. casserole; top with crumbs. Bake at 350 for 30 minutes, or until bubbling.
Variations: use chicken instead of tuna. Use cheddar cheese, cream of celery, mushroom, or chicken soup in place of cream of vegetable soup.
And—at the end, you can crush up some potato chips and put on top for the last 10 minutes or so of baking, instead of bread crumbs.

Turtle, Oven Baked

(This is from one of the Cannon relatives in Iowa, but it sounds like the Ace Bar's Snapping Turtle)
1 turtle, cut into serving pieces
Flour, seasoning salt, pepper, oil, 3 cans cream of mushroom soup, 2 soup cans milk, potatoes, cubed, carrots, diced, 1 small onion, chopped.
Soak turtle meat in salt water overnight. Rinse well.
Season flour to taste with the seasoning salt and pepper.
In a skillet, heat the oil. Roll the turtle in the flour and brown on all sides.
In a large bowl, mix the soup and milk together really well.
Place the meat in a Dutch oven and cover it with the soup mixture.
Bake at 350 degrees for 2-3 hours depending on the size of your turtle.
Half way through the baking time, add the potatoes, carrots and onion. Resume baking until the potatoes and carrots are done.
Serve using the soup mixture as gravy.

Wild Rice Hot Dish

Pour 4 cups boiling water over ½ cup white and ½ cup wild rice and let stand at least 15 minutes. (Now this is an interesting way to make rice—I use an electric rice cooker; perfect every time. Also, wild rice takes a long time to cook. I usually buy it in a can already cooked, but the baking should do the trick.)
Sauté briefly ¾ cup chopped celery, 6 Tbsp. chopped onion & 8 oz. fresh or canned mushrooms in ¼ cup butter.
Add while sautéing: 1 bay leaf crumbled, and season to taste with garlic power, pepper, onion and/or celery salt (about ¼ tsp. each)
Drain rice (if necessary) and put into a 9x13 pan.
Add 1 can each: cream of mushroom soup and cream of chicken soup, and 2 chicken bouillon cubes dissolved in 1 cup water. Mix well.
Add sautéed vegetables.
Top with Pork chops or chicken breasts, and bake covered at 350 for 1 ½ hours.
Turn meat and stir rice half way during baking.
Optional: you may use 1 ½ pounds hamburger instead of chicken or pork, and top with ½ cup slivered almonds, if desired.

Soups

Bami Soup

(Marsha Celosse)

Use oriental flavor ramen noodle soup packets and make soup as directed on the package, but use more water, so it has a lot of liquid.

Serve soup over rice with cut up raw celery, green onions, sliced boiled eggs, and dried onions.

Use ground fresh chili paste, and sweet soy sauce (ketjap manis) for flavorings.

Bean Soup

(Gloria's Navy Bean Soup that was Gene's favorite food of all time)

1 pound bag of navy beans, sorted (sometimes there are little stones)

Cover beans with water and soak overnight. In the morning, pour off water and add fresh water along with a meaty ham bone or pork hock. Add a bay leaf and cook for several hours until meat falls off the bones. Discard bones and the bay leaf.

Add 1 cup of chopped celery, 1 cup of chopped onion, 1 chopped carrot.

Add more water if needed. Simmer the rest of the day (total cooking can be 5-6 hours). Sprinkle with snipped parsley at the end and add some pepper. This is always better the second day after the flavors have really blended.

Black Soup (Rawon)

(Doeschka Schmidt) This is real Indonesian cooking! If you want to cheat like I do, buy a Rawon soup mix at the Chinese store, but here's the real thing.

2 black nuts/fruit (Kluweks); Tamarind; shrimp paste (Trassi); turmeric (kunir); ½ onion; 3 cloves garlic; salt to taste; 2 stalks of lemon grass (sereh); 3 large Indonesian bay leaves (daon salam); 2 slices of Laos (an Indonesian root).

1 ox tail or 1 pound chuck roast, cut into pieces.

Fill a pot with water and put in the meat and a bouillon of salt and tamarind. When boiling, turn heat to low. Add laos, lemon grass, daon salam and kunir and let it simmer.

Turn up soup and check that the meat is tender. When tender, take it out and cut into little cubes and put back into the soup.

Blend onion and garlic and trassi in blender. Sauté the mixture in 1 ½ tbsp. oil until aroma starts hitting your nose. Add this to the soup when the meat is tender. Let simmer for another 30 minutes.

If you like, save some of the cooked meat. Tenderize the chunks of cooked meat and marinate in a bowl of water, salt, tamarind, and garlic powder for ½ hour. Ready to be deep fried and drained, then serve on the side with the soup.

Broccoli Cream Soup

(Gloria) makes about 8 cups of soup
14 oz. pkg. frozen broccoli (about 5 cups)
1 small onion, chopped
3 cups chicken broth (the low-sodium canned stuff is great)
1 tsp. dried parsley flakes (or fresh if you have it)
¾ cup fat free half and half, and ½ cup milk
1 tbsp. cornstarch
1/8 tsp. cayenne pepper/salt to taste (be careful; there's salt in the broth)
1 tsp. garlic powder (or 1 clove of fresh garlic)
1 cup small fresh broccoli florets
1 tbsp. lemon juice

Simmer the frozen broccoli, onion, broth, and parsley for 45 minutes. Set aside to cool a little, and you can puree it in a blender in small batches. I use a potato masher instead, as we like the small lumps.

Mix the cornstarch with the milk and cream in a big pan, then add the pureed soup and everything else. Cover and simmer for another 15 minutes.

Cauliflower Cheese Soup

(Marjanne VanDemmeltraadt)
Simmer for 30 minutes:
1 small head cauliflower (cut up)
1 grated carrot
½ cup chopped celery
2 chicken bouillon cubes, 2 cups water
Cheese sauce:
Make a white sauce with 3 Tbsp. butter, 3 Tbsp. flour, salt, pepper, 2 cups milk. Stir in 1 cup shredded cheddar cheese, let cheese melt, add to soup.

Chicken Soup

3 cans low salt chicken broth
2 chicken bouillon cubes, 2 cups water
3 large carrots, diced, 3 ribs celery, diced, 1 bunch green onions, sliced
2 cups cooked chicken, diced
2 tsp. parsley, chopped, 1 tsp. chives, chopped, black pepper—no extra salt needed
1 tsp minced garlic, 2 Tbsp. real bacon bits
Simmer all about 45 minutes to an hour. If wanted, add some cooked rice or noodles when serving.

Chicken Wild Rice Soup—Low Fat

(Gloria—I make this often to take to shut-in folks. It's much enjoyed.)
Sauté briefly in 2 Tbsp. olive oil:
1 cup sliced celery
1 cup sliced carrots
1 medium onion, chopped
Add 3 Tbsp. flour
¼ tsp. pepper, dash of salt
2 cups cooked wild rice (make it ahead, or this comes precooked in cans and is great! I usually use 1 can of wild rice and 1 cup of regular rice)
1 ½ cups water (more if needed)
1 can chicken broth (no fat, low salt)

1 can cream of chicken soup
1 cup of cut up chicken breast or some ham
Heat all to boiling, cover and simmer for 15 minutes, stirring occasionally. Stir in:
1 cup fat free cream
1/3 cup almonds, sliced and slivered (check first for allergies)
¼ cup snipped parsley
Heat through, but do not boil after the cream is added.

Chinese Chicken Soup (Soto)

(Ina Lysse, another wonderful Indo cook and Onno's cousin who passed away in 2007)

4-5 chicken breasts (on the bone) plus 4 chicken bouillon cubes and lots of water. Cook all this in a big pot and let it simmer till the chicken is done. Debone the chicken and cut the meat in small pieces, then put back in the bouillon.

Have on hand:
½ head of cabbage, shredded
2 or 3 fresh lemon grass sticks, broken in 3rds
2 bunches of green onions, cut small
3-4 cloves of minced garlic
2 Tbsp. turmeric powder
2 Tbsp. canola oil
¼ cup soy sauce
2 tsp. ginger powder
4-5 macadamia nuts, ground

Add lemon grass to the soup after chicken is deboned and cut. Fry the cut green onions and garlic in frying pan with the canola oil. Add the turmeric and ginger. Stir till all is soft, then add to the soup. Add the cabbage and soy sauce, salt and pepper to taste.

Let all of this cook for approximately 25 minutes and let cool. The Soto tastes better the next day.

Serve it over cooked rice and sprinkle cooked egg slices, fine cut celery, bean sprouts and dried fried onions. Also a little lemon juice from a fresh lemon.

Don't forget the krupuk (shrimp crackers) and sambal (hot pepper paste)!
Slamat Makan! (Indonesian for "have a good meal!")

Pea Soup

1 pound dry green split peas, rinsed and sorted (that means throw out any little stones)

In a large soup pot, combine peas with:

¼ pound diced ham (or cook up a meaty ham bone in a big pot filled with water first, debone it and dice up the meat. You can also let the ham water cool overnight and throw away the congealed fat from the top before you finish making the soup.)

1 chicken bouillon cube

1 chopped onion, 1 clove minced garlic, 1 diced carrot, 1 diced celery stick, and 1 diced potato.

Salt and pepper to taste (little salt if you're using ham, and remember that the bouillon cube is salty, too). Sprinkle some cut parsley on top at the end.

At least 6-8 cups of water and you may want to add more.

Boil gently until all is tender, at least an hour or 2. Top with croutons if desired or serve with Carlotta's spicy oyster crackers.

Tomato Soup

(Gloria and Onno's adjustments to a recipe from Carlotta Neutzling in the 1970's.)

1 jar of old canned tomatoes that I made last year for the Washington County fair

2 cans of chicken broth

1 bay leaf (later discarded)

A tiny bit of sugar

Some garlic (I use minced garlic in a jar)

Salt and pepper

A glob of dried parsley (I dry this for the fair, too, and keep a baggie of it in the cupboard and use in everything)

1 pound of ground sausage—browned and crumbled and then put into the soup

Sautéed together and then put into the soup: diced onion—a lot diced celery—a few ribs a whole bunch of diced fresh tomatoes from my garden that has crop failure except for 2 large and prolific tomato plants

I make a roux of butter and flour toward the end, and add some milk to sort of thicken it a little and make it a little bit creamy. Add a few snips of parsley.

That's it and it is nummy! Thanks for the recipe so long ago!

(Note to Carlotta) The sausage gives it some bite and tastes wonderful. I never heard of sausage in tomato soup but Onno says the Dutch use it all the time and it is really good. We remembered the wonderful taste and I tried to recreate the recipe when we got home (see the next recipe). Then I found your old recipe and we liked the seasonings that you use and decided to experiment.

Tomato Soup, Dutch style

(Gloria-this is what saved my life when I was frozen at Kirkenhoff, the beautiful gardens in Holland. Onno and I remembered the taste and recreated this recipe when we got home.)
In large soup pot,
2 cans tomato soup
2 cans water
Sauté in fry pan:
3-4 sliced green onions
3 Tbsp. cooked bacon bits
2 Tbsp. sliced mushrooms
4 cooked sausage links, sliced thin (have also used a Polish kielbasa, or regular ground sausage, browned)
2 whole tomatoes, diced
Sprinkle with parsley and chives
Add all to pot of soup, stir and heat through, cook for another 5 minutes.

Tortellini Soup

(Marsha Celosse) This is a favorite of everybody who eats it! I freeze leftovers and it's great the 2nd time around, too.
1 pound Italian sausage—browned
1 large can beef bouillon (or 6 cups of water and 7 bouillon cubes)
2 large cans diced tomatoes (or fresh tomatoes)
1 can tomato sauce, 1 zucchini, diced, 1 large carrot, diced
1 green pepper, diced, 1 large onion, diced, 1 Tbsp. oregano
2 cloves minced garlic, 1 Tbsp. basil
1 tsp. dried parsley, pepper and very little salt (taste first)
Cook all in large soup pot for about 45 minutes. At the end, add 1 package tortellini, and cook for 10 more minutes. (you can also cook tortellini separately and add to the soup if you like)

Wild Rice Soup

(Shirley Rau)
½ cup cooked wild rice (canned is great)
Sauté together: 4 slices diced bacon, and 1 medium chopped onion.
1 can cream of potato soup
1 can cream of chicken soup
4 cups milk
1 cup grated American cheese
Simmer all together for 8 minutes, stirring constantly.

Vegetables, Sauces, and Salads

Baked Potatoes

Wash nice sized baking potatoes
Cut in half.
Sprinkle one side with garlic salt, butter on the other
Put a slice of onion in the middle.
Wrap in foil and bake at 350 for 1 hour

Baked Beans

(from Shirley Rau originally—Sharon VanDemmeltraadt also makes great beans and she adds a pound of browned ground beef to this basic recipe)
1 can each of Butter beans, lima beans, kidney beans (all drained; no liquid)
1 large can store-bought baked beans
5 slices chopped, crisply fried bacon
1 cup brown sugar
Mix all together and bake 1 hour at 350.
I also add onion, any other kind of bean I can find, and have made in the crock pot with success. The secret is to use several kinds of beans.

Black Bean and Corn Salad

(Esther LePage)
1 can black beans, drained.
1 pint (2 cups) whole kernel corn or 1 can, drained
¾ of a fresh red pepper, diced

1/3 cup mild onion, diced
2 Tbsp. olive oil, 1 clove minced garlic, ½ tsp. salt, 2 Tbsp. white wine vinegar
Part of feta cheese block (save 4 oz for end)
1 large tomato, diced
1/3 cup cut up cilantro
Black pepper to taste.

Cook the corn if fresh or frozen, and cool. Add the rest of the ingredients, then add the 4 oz. of feta cheese just before serving.

Boiled Beets with Orange Sauce

(Gloria) Okay, so Lee finally admitted that he has always *hated* boiled beets. Here's the recipe anyway, cuz I love 'em!

Boil whole fresh unpeeled beets in water till soft (if they're big it takes quite a while; check with a fork). When soft, drain—be careful because the red water stains everything—and cool with cold water. The skins will easily slip right off when the beets are cooked. Slice or dice the beets.

Sauce:
1 ½ Tbsp. corn starch, a little sugar, some salt, ½ cup orange juice (pulpy is best) 1 Tbsp. butter.

Cook in a pan till thick (about 3-5 minutes) add the beets and stir.

Broccoli

(Carlotta Neutzling)
2 bags of frozen broccoli—thawed
1 pound processed cheese, 1 bag of small snack crackers
1 stick butter

Spread broccoli in a baking pan. Slice cheese and cover the broccoli. Crush the crackers (put them in a plastic bag and roll with a rolling pin to crush) and pour over the cheese. Melt the butter and pour over all.

Bake 30 minutes uncovered at 350

Brushetta

4-5 tomatoes, diced (if the tomatoes are too juicy, squeeze a little of the juice and seeds into the garbage before you dice them; some tomatoes are more meaty)
1 small bunch green onions, chopped
Parsley, chives, garlic, basil, salt, pepper
1 Tbsp. extra virgin olive oil, 1 Tbsp. balsamic vinegar
Serve on small pieces of toast, or use with chips as a salsa.

Cabbage/Cauliflower Salad

(Shirley Rau)
1 head cauliflower cut in very small pieces, 1 head green cabbage, shredded
Diced onion if you like
1 pound cut up and browned bacon, crisp (add this right before serving)
Dressing:
2 cups real mayonnaise (that's one whole small 16 ounce jar)
1/3 cup grated parmesan cheese, 1/2 cup sugar, salt and pepper to taste
Put vegetables in very large bowl. Put dressing on top but don't stir. Refrigerate overnight. Add bacon and stir when ready to serve.
Lasts several days and stays crisp.

Cabbage, Irish

2 ½ pounds potatoes, peeled and cubed
4 slices bacon, ½ small head cabbage, chopped, 1 onion, chopped
½ cup milk, Salt and pepper to taste
¼ cup melted butter
Put potatoes in saucepan with water to cover. Boil until tender, about 15 minutes. Cook bacon in skillet; drain, reserve drippings, crumble the bacon and set aside. In drippings, sauté cabbage and onion until soft and translucent, about 8 minutes. Drain potatoes; mash with milk. Add salt, pepper, bacon, cabbage and onions. Transfer to serving bowl. Make a well in center and pour in butter. Serves about 8.

Caramel Apple Salad

(Linda Bergen, makes about 6 servings)
1 small pkg. instant vanilla pudding
1 1/3 cups milk
4 oz. whipped topping
2 apples, diced
2 chocolate/caramel candy bars, diced
Blend pudding and milk. Add whipped topping and mix until smooth. Stir in apples and candy. Chill until ready to serve.

Cauliflower, Tangy Mustard

1 medium head of cauliflower (can be used whole, or cut up; takes longer to cook whole, but looks fancier. I prefer to cut it up)

Cook cauliflower in microwave with a little water, or steam it, or boil on stove, as preferred—don't cook too long as to be mushy.

Combine:

½ cup real mayonnaise, 1 Tbsp. minced onion, 1 tsp. yellow mustard

Spoon sauce over cauliflower and sprinkle with shredded cheese as desired. Nuke on medium power for 2 minutes to melt cheese.

Cheesy Potatoes

(Gloria) I've combined several recipes and this is different each time I make it, but these are the basics.

2 pound package frozen, cubed hash browns
½ cup melted butter
A small diced onion or more if you like (or leave it out if you have picky kids)
1 can cream soup (mushroom, celery . . .)
1 cup sour cream
1 cup milk
8 oz. shredded cheddar (or whatever cheese you like)
4 to 8 oz. grated mozzarella cheese
Salt and pepper to taste (careful with the salt, the cheese and soup are salty)

Mix all ingredients well and spread into greased casserole. Bake at 350 for 1-1 ½ hours or until bubbly and browned.

Corn Casserole

(Cannon reunion 1980's—the Cannon family favorite)
1 can whole kernel corn (drained)
1 can creamed corn
1 package 8.5 oz Jiffy ® corn bread muffin mix
1 stick butter, melted, 1 8-ounce container sour cream, 1 egg

Mix all together well, bake in greased glass bowl at 350 for 45 minutes, till golden brown and cracked on top (like muffins).

Corn-Cheese Bake

1 16 ounce can cream style corn
1 16 ounce can whole kernel corn, drained
1/3 cup flour
1 3 ounce package cream cheese, cut in cubes
½ tsp onion salt
½ cup shredded Swiss cheese (2 ounces)

Stir flour into creamed corn. Add cream cheese and onion. Heat and stir till cheese melts. Stir in remaining ingredients. Pour into 1 1/2 quart casserole, top with buttered bread crumbs, if desired. Bake uncovered at 400 for 30 minutes. Serves 6-8.

Cucumbers

(Mary Lou Titus)
Slice cucumbers and soak in cold salt water for a few hours, drain.
Add some sliced onions, a little vinegar, sugar, salt and pepper to taste.

Dill Pickles

(Gloria from the farm days)
Brine for 2 quarts of pickles. Boil this and pour over the cucumbers packed in hot jars:
3 cups water
1 cup white vinegar
¼ cup canning salt
Cucumbers: Soak in water overnight.

(Wear rubber gloves, this stuff is hot!) In the bottom of clean, hot jars, place a good sprig of dill and 1 clove of garlic. Pack the cukes on top of this. Pour boiling brine to ½ inch from top of jar. Put on hot lids (always use new lids and use them straight out of boiling water) and rings, and let cool, tightening rings as it cools.

These have always sealed without canning for me, if everything is hot enough. If desired (or if you're exhibiting them at the county fair) you can boil the filled jars in the canner for 20 minutes.

Dried Parsley/chives/cilantro/mint, etc.

(Gloria's county fair blue ribbon dried herbs)
Use fresh herbs either purchased or grown in pots or your garden. Wash the herbs in cool water and leave pretty wet. Using kitchen scissor, cut in very small pieces onto a large paper towel, and discard stems. Lift towel carefully and put in the microwave. Nuke at 30 second intervals on high; takes about 2 minutes per batch to dry completely, but watch carefully because it can burn easily (I've had one batch burst into flame!). Remove and store tightly to keep dry (plastic bags or jars). Herbs stay green this way and keep smelling really fresh for a long time. This makes a lovely hostess gift, useful and pretty.

Freezing Fresh Corn

8 cups of raw corn cut off the cob (it works to put the cob in the hole in the center of an angel food pan, then use a knife to slice off the kernels down into the pan and the pieces don't fly all over)
¼ cup butter, 2 Tbsp. sugar, 1 tsp. salt, 1 cup water
Cook all for barely 2 minutes, cool and freeze in packages.

Gado Gado-Indonesian Salad

(from all of the Indo ladies—everyone makes it)
This is basically cabbage salad—use enough of each ingredient for the number of people you have. All items can be room temperature, but the peanut sauce should be warm.
Cabbage—shredded and cooked till almost done
Green beans (canned, fresh or frozen, but fresh is better) cook till almost done
Boiled potatoes—sliced
Hard boiled eggs—sliced
Cucumber slices
Bean sprouts
Fried tofu (optional)
Serve with warm peanut sauce as a "dressing" and put crispy dried onion rings (canned) on top. Also serve with krupuk (shrimp crackers)

Green Bean Casserole

(Cannon favorite, Sue Cannon makes it best)
2 regular cans of cream of mushroom soup
1 cup milk

2 tsp. soy sauce, ¼ tsp. black pepper
8 cups cooked cut green beans (you can use canned or frozen)
1 can of dried/fried onions

Stir soup, milk, soy sauce, pepper, beans and ½ of the dried onions in a 3 qt. casserole. Bake at 350 for 25 minutes or until hot. Stir, and top with remaining onions. Bake for 5 minutes more, till browned.

Hutspot—Dutch Potatoes and Carrots

(Marjanne VanDemmeltraadt)
Equal parts (about 1 pound of each) peeled potatoes and carrots, cut in small chunks. Diced onion, if desired. 1 tsp. salt, ¼ tsp mace.
Boil everything together with water to barely cover, till done.
Drain and mash with milk, butter, salt, and a dash of mace.
Serve with sausage (Polish sausage, or brats).

Katie's Potatoes

(somebody from Carlotta Neutzling's family)
6-8 medium potatoes, partially boiled without skins and grated. Or take the easy way out and use frozen hash browns.
Fill a 9x13 pan with the potatoes. Pour ½ pint cream over the potatoes and cut up ½ stick butter on top. Bake 30-40 minutes at 350. You can also add chopped onions and a little cheese on top if you like, and salt and pepper to taste.

Macaroni Salad

7-8 oz. pkg. macaroni, cooked, cooled in cold water, and drained (if you add a little butter to the boiling water, it won't boil over, however, if you add butter the sauce doesn't stick as well, so it's your choice).
In large bowl, add:
1/3 cup chopped onion
1 cup chopped celery
1 cup lightly cooked frozen peas
1 tsp. dried parsley (or fresh if you have it)
1 cup diced meat (chicken, tuna, ham or . . . .)
Diced cheese is optional, too
Mix together with the macaroni and some mayonnaise dressing till moist (about 1 cup)
Season as desired with salt/pepper/seasoned salt/maybe some celery seed
Best if made the day before and cooled overnight to blend the flavors.

Mashed Potato Cakes

(Marjanne VanDemmeltraadt)
2 cups seasoned mashed potatoes (you can used packaged or real)
1 egg, lightly beaten, 1 tsp. chopped onion, 1 tsp. parsley
Combine all, shape into round cakes about ¾" thick. Brown in hot oil on both sides.

Peanut Sauce

(Elly Mettler)
1 small onion, minced
2 Tbsp. oil
1 or 2 tsp. sambal (hot pepper paste)
1-2 tsp. garlic powder or 1-2 cloves of minced garlic)
12 Tbsp. peanut butter (chunky or creamy)
6 Tbsp. ketjap manis (sweet soy sauce)
2 Tbsp. coconut milk, dry or canned
1 tsp. brown sugar
A little lemon juice
Slowly brown onion and garlic in oil. Add hot pepper paste and peanut butter and mix well (it will be thick) add boiling water until thick, smooth sauce. (it will get really thick and orange colored, but keep slowly adding water). Simmer for a few minutes. Add the sweet soy sauce, coconut milk, sugar, lemon juice. Taste and add salt if needed.

Gloria's version: I buy packets of peanut sauce in the Asian section and make as directed . . .

Potato Casserole

(Shirley Allen's friend Dorothy from California)
10 medium potatoes, boiled in salted water till tender. Mash and add:
1 cup sour cream
1 cup cottage cheese
½ cup butter
1 Tbsp. grated onion, 1 tsp. salt, ¼ tsp. pepper.
Put in greased casserole, top with ¼ cup grated parmesan cheese.
Bake at 325-350 for 45+ minutes. This can be made ahead and refrigerated until you bake it.

Pumpkin

(Gloria) unusual—and good—accompaniment to a fall dinner. I served with meal of pork and potatoes and a green salad. Got this recipe from a lady shopping at the same pumpkin stand when we got to talking. I went home and tried it—nummy!

Hollow out a small pumpkin for each 2 people.

Stuff with:

Cut up apples, pineapple tidbits, dried apricot, dried cranberries, raisins, cinnamon, nutmeg, butter, brown sugar.

Start it in the microwave for a few minutes, then bake at 350 for about an hour.

Put on a plate between 2 people and each can scoop out as much as they want. It's pretty, nutritious, and tastes good, too!

Ramen Noodle Salad

(Joan Johnson)

2 packages oriental flavor ramen noodle soup mix; break up the noodles (save spice for dressing)

4 cups shredded cabbage (Napa cabbage is best)

1/3 cup shredded carrots

1 bunch green onions, chopped

½ cup water chestnuts, sliced

1 cup toasted, slivered almonds

1 cup sunflower seeds

Dressing:

¾ cup sugar

½ cup apple cider vinegar

¼ cup olive oil

2 packets of seasoning from ramen noodles

Mix dressing 2 hours before serving

Just before serving: mix vegetables together, then pour dressing over and mix well. For crunchier salad, add ramen noodles right before serving.

Tomatoes

(Shirley Rau)
Fresh tomatoes, sliced—about 4-5, ½ cup oil, 2 Tbsp. cider vinegar
2 Tbsp. sugar, 1 ½ tsp. crushed basil, ¼ tsp. dry mustard
Salt and pepper to taste, 1 tsp. garlic powder (or minced garlic)
Sprinkle of parsley, 1 large onion, sliced
Layer tomatoes and onions with marinade; marinate at room temperature for 2-3 hours.

Vegetable Hot Dish

(Minnesota's name) or **Vegetable Casserole** (from any other part of the country) (Sharon Dornfeld)
2—1 lb bags of frozen broccoli, carrots & cauliflower; nuke on high 5 minutes.
2 cans cream of mushroom soup
1 cup shredded cheddar cheese
Put soup and cheese in pan on stove until cheese melts. Pour over vegetables. Bake 30 minutes or until bubbly. Remove from oven and sprinkle 1 can dried/fried onion rings over top. Return to oven bake until onion rings are brown about 5-10 minutes.

Desserts

Almond Puff

(Mary Weise) Special treat for lazy farm days
½ cup butter (1 stick), 1 cup flour, 2 Tbsp. water
Mix with fork, divide in ½; pat in 2 (12x3) strips on ungreased cookie sheet.
Heat another ½ cup butter and 1 cup water to boil, then remove.
Stir in 1 tsp. almond extract and 1 cup flour. Stir over low heat till it forms a ball. Remove and beat in 3 eggs until smooth.
Spread over the 2 strips, covering each completely.
Bake 60 minutes at 350. Glaze.
Glaze:
1 ½ cups powdered sugar, 2 Tbsp. soft butter, 1 tsp. almond extract, 1-2 Tbsp. warm water.
Stir and drizzle on baked strips, then sprinkle with sliced almonds.

Angel Cookies

(Gloria)—I found at least 4 copies of this on various sorts of messy paper in Lee's little boy handwriting—I think he liked them.
Cream together:
1 cup butter (2 sticks), ½ cup white sugar, ½ cup brown sugar
Add:
1 egg, 1 tsp. vanilla, 1 tsp. soda, 1 tsp. cream of tartar, dash of salt
2 ¼ cups flour
Mix well; roll in small balls. Press with glass dipped in sugar (rub bottom of glass with butter and then dip in sugar).
Bake at 350 for 10 minutes on greased cookie sheets

Angel Food Cake Endless Possibilities

(Gloria got from a friend at Lake Elmo Curves for Women)

1 box of 1-step angel food cake mix. Use any variations in the list below.

Preheat oven to 350. Mix the angel food cake mix and desired flavor ingredients together and beat by hand until blended. Pour into ungreased 9x13 pan (or muffin tins) and bake for 35-40 minutes (muffins bake 15-18 minutes). Cool upside down for best results.

Lemon: 1 C + 3 T water, 2 T lemon juice and 2 tsp. grated lemon peel

Orange Citrus: 1-1/4 C water and 2 t grated orange peel

Cherry: 1 can (20 oz) light cherry pie filling

Black Forest: add ½ cup cocoa to cherry version

Cotton Candy: 1 small (3.4 oz) sugar-free gelatin, any flavor, 1-1/4 C water.

Margarita: 1 C+ 2 T water, 2 T fresh lime juice and 1-1/2 tsp. grated lime rind

Pineapple: 1 (20 oz) crushed pineapple with juice (*this is great*)

Pina Colada: add 1 T each coconut & rum extracts to pineapple directions

Apple Sauce

(Gloria) I made up this recipe after using Morgan's apples. Num!

Peel, core, and cut up a big pan full of at least 3 different kinds of apples for the best taste. You can use one kind, of course, but using a variety does make a difference.

Add a little water, maybe 1 1/2 cups or so for a big pan full of apples

Add cinnamon, at least 1 heaping tsp. and a handful of red-hot cinnamon candies.

Add a handful of fresh cranberries and a dash of lemon juice.

Cook all till the apples are tender, but not mushy. Then add a little sugar to taste.

Don't add sugar until the apples have cooked down, because you don't want to get it too sweet. Add 1 Tbsp at a time of any sort of sugar; brown, natural or white. It doesn't take much. If it gets too sweet, add more lemon juice.

This freezes well and lasts a long time in the refrigerator. Serve with meats, like pork.

Apple Crisp

(Diane Morgan)
3 cups flour, 3 cups sugar
1 1/2 tsp. cinnamon, 1/2 tsp nutmeg, 2 1/2 sticks butter
Crumble and put on top of enough apples to fill a greased 9 x 13 pan.
Bake at 350 until done

Note from Diane: This couldn't be any easier. It's my favorite apple crisp recipe. Remember to use at least three or more different kinds of apples to get the best flavor. We are lucky that we have our own orchard so the selection is exceptional.

Bananas, Fried

(Karen Cannon Ellefson from early school years)
Per Karen: "Fried bananas were simple (although mine tasted awful!) Cut up, sprinkle with paprika and fry briefly in butter until lightly browned and enjoy!"

In more recent years, Onno and I had fried bananas in Indonesia that were wonderful. The difference might be the kind of bananas, and they were in a batter and deep fried with powdered sugar on top; really good. You can use plantains, also which we ate in the jungles near the Panama Canal.

Boter Koek (Shortbread Cookies)

(Corrie Stulen—this recipe was originally from Holland and in metric measurements. I converted it)
½ cup butter (1 stick) (125 grams)
½ cup sugar (125 grams)
1 ¼ cup flour (150 grams)
A small pinch of salt
½ beaten egg (break an egg into a dish and beat well; pour ½ into the batter and save ½ for later.)

Mix all well and press into 8 inch round or square pan (buttered and floured)

Press into the top: slivered almonds or sliced candied ginger. (Corrie always makes one of each. Onno likes the ginger, and I like the almond.)

Brush the rest of the beaten egg on top of all, and bake at 350 for 25-30 minutes.

Brownies-1

(Gloria—this is the one that I was "told" to bring to every gathering in the '70s-80's)

½ cup dry cocoa, ½ cup boiling water, ½ cup butter, ½ cup margarine
2 cups sugar, 3 eggs, 2 cups flour, ½ cup milk, 1 cup chopped nuts
1 tsp. vanilla

Add cocoa to boiling water, cool. Cream butter, margarine and sugar; beat in eggs. Add cocoa mixture. Add flour and milk alternately; beat well. Add nuts and vanilla. Bake at 350 in jelly roll pan for 30 minutes. Yield: 3-4 dozen.

Frosting:
1/3 cup milk, 1 cup sugar, 1 square chocolate, ¼ cup butter, dash of salt
Boil all ingredients for 1 minute. Beat until spreading consistency. Spread over brownies.

Brownies-2

Melt together over low heat and set aside:
14 ounces of caramels (unwrapped), 1/3 cup evaporated milk
Mix together:
1 package German chocolate cake mix
¾ cup butter or margarine, 1/3 cup evaporated milk, 1 cup chopped nuts
Press ½ of this mixture into 9x13 pan (greased)
Bake 8 minutes at 350.
Sprinkle 6 ounces of chocolate chips (about 1 cup) over the hot bars.
Spread the caramel mixture over all. Crumble the remaining ½ of the cake mixture over this. Bake 15-20 minutes at 350. Cool completely.

Brownies-3

(Hazel Shigley)
1 stick butter, 1 cup sugar, 4 eggs, 1 tsp. vanilla
1 can chocolate syrup (16 ounce can)
1 cup + 2 Tbsp. flour, ¾ cup chopped walnuts
Mix together and bake in 12x15 greased jelly roll pan, 30 minutes at 350.
Frosting:
1 stick butter, 6 Tbsp. milk, 1 ½ cups sugar

Boil 1 minute after it starts bubbling good. Add ½ cup chocolate chips and beat well. Pour over brownies while hot.

Hazel says, "I usually start frosting 5 minutes before brownies are done. The frosting sets up real fast, so dump the pan full on the brownies and spread quickly."

Butter Balls

(Gloria) Made for Christmas for many, many years.
1 cup soft butter, ½ cup powdered sugar, 1 tsp. vanilla, ¼ tsp. salt
2/3 cup chopped nuts (walnuts or pecans), 2 ¼ cups flour
Mix well with fork. Shape dough into balls. Bake 10 minutes at 400. Roll baked balls in powdered sugar (may do this twice).

Butter Mochi

(Susan, Frannie's daughter from Hawaii. Delicious!)
1 pound rice flour, available in the Asian foods section, and very cheap
1 tsp. baking powder, 1 ½ cup milk, 5 eggs, 1 can coconut milk (14 oz.)
2 cups sugar, 1 tsp. vanilla, 1 stick butter, melted
Combine all except for butter. Mix well with electric mixer. Add butter last. Pour into greased or sprayed 9x13 pan. Bake at 350 for 1 hour.

Option: sprinkle top with shredded coconut before baking. Best warm out of the oven.

Caramel Popcorn

(Gloria—recovered from Renee because I forgot this was my recipe) I have given tons of this away at Christmas and everyone loves it.
5-6 quarts of popped corn (I use purchased pre-popped white popcorn—it is more tender than what you pop yourself)
I use my huge roaster pan to mix it in—this makes a large amount
Caramel sauce:
1 ½ cups white sugar, ½ cup white corn syrup, 1 cup butter
Bring caramel ingredients to a boil. Boil 10 minutes (no less or it doesn't get hard—it should be at the spin-thread stage) stirring constantly. Remove from heat and add 1 Tbsp. vanilla. Pour over popcorn and stir well. Spread onto wax paper. Can mix in some nuts if desired. Let cool, break apart and store in tight bags. Makes a really nice house gift when going for dinner.

Chocolate Beet Cake

(Sara Cannon) She made this for Henry's 3rd birthday party and everybody loved it! It's also the only way that Lee will eat beets.

1 ¼ cups beet puree (boil beets and blend or use food processor to puree)

3 eggs, ½ cup vegetable oil, ¾ cup dry cocoa, 1 ½ cups sugar, 1 tsp. vanilla, 1 ½ cups flour, 1 ½ tsp. baking soda, ½ tsp. salt.

Grease and flour a round fluted pan or 9" square pan. Beat eggs and add wet ingredients. Mix dry ingredients and then add to wet stuff.

Pour into pan and bake at 350 for 45-50 minutes.

Frosting:

1 stick softened butter, 4 ounces soft cream cheese, 2 cups powdered sugar, 2/3 cup dry cocoa, 1 tsp. vanilla.

Mix well with electric mixer and frost the cake (no cooking!)

Chocolate Cherry Bars

1 package chocolate fudge cake mix

21 ounce can cherry pie filling, 1 tsp. almond extract (or vanilla), 2 eggs

Mix all together well. Bake in greased 9x13 pan at 350 for 30-35 minutes.

Frosting:

1 cup sugar, 5 T butter, 1/3 cup milk

Boil one minute and add 1 cup chocolate chips, stir till smooth, then spread on cooled bars.

Chocolate Chip Oatmeal Bars

Fast, easy treat for hungry kids after school

1 cup butter, 1 cup packed brown sugar, 1 cup white sugar

2 eggs, 1 1/3 cup oatmeal, 1 2/3 cup flour

1 small package chocolate chips (6 ounce)

1 tsp. soda, 1 tsp. vanilla, 1 tsp. water

Mix all together and put in greased 9x13 pan. Bake at 350 for 30 minutes.

Chocolate Frosting

(Jan Grone) Mom would put this on a white cake or a chocolate one, or brownies.
Melt ¼ cup butter. Add ½ cup dry cocoa, ¼ tsp. salt
Stir in 1/3 cup milk, 1 ½ tsp. vanilla.
Put 3 ½ cups powdered sugar in bowl and mix with chocolate mixture. Beat until creamy (may have to add more milk)
Add dash of mint flavoring if desired.

Club® Cracker Cookies

(Marsha Celosse & Gloria) These are wonderful!
42 Club® crackers (exactly 1 sleeve from a box of regular Keebler ® Club ® crackers (© Kellogg Co.)
Lay the crackers out evenly on a jelly roll pan (large cookie sheet with sides). I like to line the pan with foil as it's very messy and if you don't get them out of the pan right away at the end, they harden and you'll have problems. If you don't use foil, do not grease pan. Just be sure to remove cookies immediately after baking).
In a sauce pan, boil for 2 minutes:
¾ cup (1 ½ sticks) butter, ½ cup sugar
After boiling, add 1 tsp. vanilla
Pour evenly over crackers. Sprinkle about ½ to ¾ cup sliced almonds or pecans on top. Bake for 10-12 minutes at 350. Remove from pan immediately to wire rack while still very hot. Cool and store tightly to keep crisp.

Fudge

(Paula Quinlan brings this to holiday gatherings and it's nummy.)
2/3 cup butter (not margarine!!!)
3 cups sugar (buy fresh for best results)
2/3 cups evaporated milk (not condensed milk)
1 package of milk chocolate chips (12 ounce)
1 jar of marshmallow crème (7 ounce)
1 tsp vanilla
1 cup chopped nuts if desired and you don't have allergies (walnuts, pecans, macadamia, the choice is endless)
Melt butter, add milk, bring to boil, add sugar, boil for 5 minutes, stirring constantly with rolling boil (yes, keep stirring or it will scorch, yuck!). Add chocolate chips and stir until melted. Add marshmallow crème, stir until melted. Add nuts. Pour into 8" x 8" lightly buttered pan, cool, lick spoon and enjoy!

Fattigmand

(Hazel Shigley)
6 eggs, well beaten, pinch of salt, 1 tsp. vanilla
6 Tbsp. sweet cream, 6 tsp. sugar, 2 cups flour
Mix all together, roll out with rolling pin. Cut in triangular shapes and fry in deep fat like doughnuts.

Granola Bars

(from a Ladies Ensemble member, Eunice Lodoen in 1979)
3 ½ cup oats (any kind)
1 cup raisins, 1 cup chopped nuts
1/3 cup butter
½ cup brown sugar
1/3 cup honey, corn syrup, or molasses
1 beaten egg, ½ tsp. salt, and ½ tsp. vanilla
Toast oats in ungreased large shallow pan; 350 oven 15-20 minutes
Combine toasted oats with remaining ingredients. Mix well and press firmly in greased jelly roll pan (large cookie sheet with sides). Bake at 350 for 20 minutes, cool and cut into bars.

Grapes

(Marsha Celosse) This has some fancy French name also and Marsha says that it's served as a dessert at very fine restaurants.
Fresh Green grapes
Sour cream and brown sugar.
Wash grapes and dry well with paper towels. Put some sour cream in a dish, add grapes and stir so each is coated. Then sprinkle well with brown sugar or roll grapes in another bowl with brown sugar. Serve in fancy dishes; very pretty and nummy.

Key Lime Pie

(Diane Morgan)
3 egg yolks
1 can sweetened condensed milk
½ bottle (4 oz) lime juice
Beat all until blended. Pour into graham cracker pie crust. Bake for 30 minutes at 325. Put meringue on top or whipped cream.

Krumkake

(Shirley Bird—there are lots of recipes for Norwegian Krumkake, Shirley makes it best. You need a special Krumkake iron to make this.)

2 eggs, beaten, 1 cup sugar, ½ cup soft butter
1 cup (scant) milk, 1 ½ cups flour, 1 tsp. cardamom

Beat all together. Heat krumkake iron till drop of water sizzles on it. Brush plates lightly with butter, drop batter onto iron by 1 Tbsp. Take baked cookie off iron and roll onto stick.

Lemon Bars 1

Cut ½ cup butter into 1 cup flour and ¼ cup powdered sugar
Press into 11x7 pan (or 9x9), bake 15 minutes at 325.
Mix together:
1 cup sugar, 2 Tbsp. flour, ½ tsp. baking powder, dash of salt
2 beaten eggs, 2 Tbsp. lemon juice, 1 tsp. lemon rind
Spread over baked crust. Bake 25 minutes at 325. Cool and glaze.
Glaze:
½ cup powdered sugar, 1 Tbsp. lemon juice, 1 Tbsp. melted butter
A drop of yellow food color if you want it to look really lemony.

Lemon Bars 2

(Gloria—I was requested to bring these to lots of gatherings—I always doubled the recipe to fit a 9x13 pan)

Mix ½ cup butter, 1 cup flour, ¼ cup powdered sugar, and pat into 9-inch square pan. Bake at 350 for 15 minutes.
Mix and pour over hot crust:
2 Tbsp. lemon juice, 2 beaten eggs, 2 Tbsp. flour
2 tsp. grated lemon rind
1 cup sugar, ½ tsp. baking powder
Bake at 350 for 25 minutes. Sprinkle with powdered sugar or frost. Makes 16 bars.
Lemon glaze:
2 cups powdered sugar, 1 Tbsp. butter, juice of 1 lemon
Combine all ingredients and mix well; spread on hot bars and cut.

Lemon Meringue Pie

(Jan Grone)
Use ½ of Jan's pie crust recipe for this single crust pie.
Filling, mix together:
6 Tbsp. corn starch, 1 ½ cup sugar, 2 ¼ cups boiling water.
Cook in double boiler until thick and starting to boil.
Add ½ tsp. salt, juice from 1 lemon and grated peel from 1 lemon.
Add beaten yolks from 4 eggs (save the whites for meringue) (good idea to mix a little of the hot mixture in the eggs before adding to the rest).
Cook 4 minutes.
Add 1 Tbsp. butter. Pour into baked crust.
Meringue: Beat whites of the 4 eggs, adding 5 or 6 Tbsp. of sugar, 1 at a time. Continue beating until peaks form. Cover the pie with the meringue being sure to get to the edge of the pan. Bake at 425 until browned. Let cool and enjoy!

Macadamia Nut Cake

Gene Cannon's "prize winner"
Grease and flour a 9x13 pan
Filling:
½ cup low-fat sweetened condensed milk (not evaporated)
½ cup dark chocolate chips
Cook in small saucepan over low heat till chocolate is melted. Set aside.
Cake:
1 package of chocolate cake mix
1 ½ tsp. cinnamon
½ cup vegetable oil
1 can (16 ounces) pears, drained and mashed until smooth
2 eggs
½ cup chopped macadamia nuts
2 tsp. water
In large bowl, blend the cake mix, cinnamon and oil at low speed until crumbly.

In another bowl, mix ½ of the crumbly cake mixture, the mashed pears, and eggs. Beat for 2 minutes. Spread batter evenly in prepared pan. Drop filling by spoonfuls over the batter. Stir nuts and water into the remaining cake mix. Sprinkle over filling.

Bake at 350 for 45-50 minutes, or till top springs back when touched lightly in center.

Sauce:

Mix 1/3 cup milk with 1 jar (17 ounces) caramel fudge ice cream topping. Either heat on stove or in microwave briefly.

Top each piece of cake with warm sauce. To make it even richer, add some vanilla ice cream on top of that.

Magic Marshmallow Puff-Ups

(Maddy Sevilla, Josie, and Katie VanDemmeltraadt made these for the Washington County Fair)

2 cans refrigerated crescent rolls; separate rolls into 16 triangles.
¼ cup sugar and 1 tsp. cinnamon
16 large marshmallows, ¼ cup melted butter
¼ cup chopped nuts (optional)

Dip a marshmallow in melted butter, then into cinnamon/sugar mixture. Wrap triangle around each marshmallow and pinch edges to seal tightly. Dip sealed sides in butter and place in deep muffin pan.

Place muffin pan on baking sheet during baking. Bake at 375 for 10-15 minutes, or until golden brown. Drizzle with icing and sprinkle with nuts, if desired.

Icing:
½ cup powdered sugar
2-3 Tbsp. milk
½ tsp. vanilla

Marzipan

(Elly Mettler)

Buy a can of almond paste (in the baking aisle) and frozen pastry sheets. Roll out the pastry sheet; roll the almond paste in your hands like a "snake" and lay on the pastry sheet. Roll it up together and put on a cookie sheet. Sprinkle with sugar and bake at 400 for about 15 minutes, or until golden. Slice in pieces to serve.

Queen Elizabeth Cake

(Gloria) This is a very old recipe (modified of course) and I heard somewhere that Queen Elizabeth II is supposed to have made the original herself. Whether she did or not, it is *royally* good!

Pour 1 cup boiling water over 1 cup chopped dates and 1 tsp. soda. Let stand.

Mix the following:
1 cup sugar, ¼ cup butter, 1 beaten egg, 1 tsp. vanilla
1 ½ cup flour, 1 tsp. baking powder, 1/4 tsp. salt, ½ cup chopped nuts
Add to date mixture and stir. Pour into greased 9x12 cake pan and bake for 35 minutes at 350.
Icing:
5 Tbsp. brown sugar, 5 Tbsp. cream, 2 Tbsp. butter.
Boil 3 minutes, spread onto cooled cake. If desired, sprinkle with coconut and nuts.

Pecans, Candied

(Ina Lysse) This is terrific and I've given away lots of them for Christmas in cute containers; nice gift.
1 pound pecan halves
1 egg white with 1 Tbsp. water
1 cup sugar, 1 tsp. salt, 1 tsp. cinnamon
Beat egg white and water till foamy in large bowl. Add pecans and stir to coat. Mix dry ingredients in a separate bowl, then add to pecans. Stir well. Bake 25 minutes at 300 in a large cookie sheet with sides. Spread out on foil to cool. Store in tight container.

Pie Crust

(Jan Grone) (makes a bottom and top crust) *The best!*
3 cups flour, 1 tsp. baking powder, 2 tsp. sugar, 1 tsp. salt,
1 ½ cup shortening (it's better with lard, but that's a no-no these days)
Mix with a fork; add 8 Tbsp very cold water and 2 Tbsp. lemon juice, a little at a time. Roll it out carefully using enough flour to not stick, and butter the bottom of the pie pan before laying the crust in it.

Plum Crunch

(Diane Morgan)
3 pounds fresh plums, quartered and pitted (5 cups)
1/4 cup brown sugar, 1 cup sifted enriched flour 1 cup granulated sugar
1/2 tsp. salt, 1/2 tsp. cinnamon, 1 beaten egg, 1/2 cup butter melted.
Combine plums and brown sugar. Spoon into 11 1/2 x 7 1/2 x 1 1/2" baking dish. Sift together dry ingredients; add egg, tossing with fork until mixture is crumbly; sprinkle evenly over plums. Drizzle with butter.

Bake in moderate oven (375) about 45 min. or until lightly browned. Serve warm topped with ice cream or whipped cream. Makes 8 servings.

Note from Diane: This is a wonderful, easy dish that I have used many times. I got the recipe from my aunt who is now 95 years old.

Pretzels with Caramels

(Gloria—got from a friend at Curves for Women—we *have* to exercise if we eat stuff like this!)

Buy a bag of regular pretzels

2 bags of chocolate covered caramel candies

On a cookie sheet, put a candy in the middle of each pretzel. Bake at 350 for 2-3 minutes until the candy is soft.

Put a pecan in the middle of the candy.

Refrigerate till firm.

Prune Kolaches

(Gloria made it up from memories and a little help from the internet)

I never ate Anna's Kolaches, but remember that they looked and smelled pretty good. I'm not including a dough recipe here because in this day and age, I'd use frozen sweet bread dough.

Thaw the dough and cut into single serving size pieces. Spread each little square out on a floured surface, make a dent in the middle and fill with Prune Filling.

Prune Filling:

1 pound dried prunes (with no pits)

1 tsp. vanilla, 1 cup sugar, 1 tsp. fresh lemon juice, 1 tsp. grated lemon peel (they call this "zest" these days).

Put the prunes in a saucepan and cover with water. Add the vanilla and simmer until the prunes have softened, about 15 minutes. Drain and chop them in a food processor or chop by hand with the sugar, lemon juice, and lemon zest.

Fill the dent in the dough with some filling, and fold the edges over the filling. It doesn't have to be sealed perfectly. Bake as directed on the dough package.

If wanted, you could drizzle a little powdered sugar frosting on the top when cooled.

Rhubarb Cake

(this is in Lee's writing—no clue where he got it)
Preheat oven to 350, grease a large cake pan.
1 white cake mix (no pudding in it); prepare mix as directed on box.
Combine 4 cups of chopped rhubarb, 1 ½ cups sugar; layer over the cake mix.
Pour 1 pint cream over the top and bake for 1 hour at 350. Serve with whipped cream.

Rosettes

(Hazel Shigley, Shirley Bird, Gloria—the recipe is simple with lots of varieties, but this one works pretty well)
2 eggs, 1 Tbsp. sugar, ¼ tsp. salt, 1 cup whole milk, 1 cup flour, 1 tsp. vanilla
Beat all till like cream. Heat oil in fryer. Heat rosette iron till hot, then dip in batter. Fry quickly. Dust with powdered sugar or regular sugar. Keep in covered container to stay crisp.

It's important that the grease is the right temperature. If too hot or not hot enough, the rosettes will be greasy.

Rum Cake

Makes 1 large cake in a fluted pan, about 12 servings. I also have made it in a 9x13 pan and it works fine, just looks fancier in a fluted cake pan.
Cake:
1 package (18.5 oz) classic yellow cake mix, 1 cup coconut rum, ½ cup vegetable oil, 1 package (3.4 oz) vanilla instant pudding mix, 4 eggs
Grease and flour pan well; heat oven to 325.
Beat all ingredients in large bowl for at least 2 minutes. Pour into pan, and bake about 45 minutes, until a toothpick is clean.
Cool cake upright in pan for 20 minutes. Invert cake onto platter and carefully remove pan. Allow cake to cool completely.
Rum Glaze:
1 cup (packed) brown sugar, ¼ cup water, 1 stick butter, ¼ cup coconut rum
Stir sugar and water in heavy pan over medium heat until sugar dissolves.
Add butter and boil gently for at least 5 minutes until mixture thickens (usually 7-8 minutes). Remove from heat and cool briefly, then stir in the rum. Cool glaze completely.
Drizzle glaze evenly over cooled cake and serve.
(I drizzle a little of the hot sauce over the cake so it really soaks in and then cool it completely and put the rest on. The sauce will thicken as it cools.)
Great with a little ice cream.

Toffee Bars

(Hazel Shigley from 1960's. I can't imagine how many pans of these I've made over the past 50 years—they're still terrific!)

1 cup butter
1 cup brown sugar
1 egg
1 tsp. vanilla, dash of salt
2 cups flour

Mix well and spread with floured hands in greased jelly roll pan.

Bake at 325 for 25 minutes. Remove from oven and pour 1 cup of milk chocolate chips over the top. Return to oven for no more than 1 minute to soften chocolate. Spread melted chocolate evenly, and cut while hot.

DRINKS

Fruit Slush

(Non-Alcohol) (Renee Cannon)
2 packages frozen strawberries
12 ounces frozen lemonade concentrate
6 ounce can frozen orange juice concentrate
1 20-ounce can crushed pineapple and juice
1 quart lemon-lime soda
Mix well in empty ice cream bucket and freeze 8-12 hours. Can add a little lemon-lime soda to serve.

Pink Vodka Slush

1 (large) can frozen pink lemonade concentrate
1 can cranberry juice
2 cans lemon-lime soda
1 can vodka (can use gin or bourbon)
Use lemonade can to measure. Combine all ingredients. Mix and freeze in a plastic container like an ice cream pail (double the recipe to fill pail). Stir every few hours until frozen. When serving, scoop some into glass and add a little lemon-lime soda or ginger ale to thaw it out a little.

Raspberry Punch

(Karen Ellefson—she describes this as beautiful and easy; perfect for a shower or fancy party, and kids love it.)
Raspberry sherbet mixed with raspberry ginger ale and a little lemon-lime soda. That's all it is; just mix in a punch bowl and enjoy! You can add an ice ring to be fancy, and maybe some real raspberries.

Fun Stuff: Notes, Reminders, Interesting Stuff, and Doo Dads

Bread Crumbs

Remove crusts from day old bread and tear bread into pieces. Put pieces into a blender or food processor and pulse on/off until you have fine crumbs.

Cough Syrup

(Carlotta Neutzling)
6 lemons, juiced
1 carton honey (6-8 ounces)
Mix and heat till runny; add 2 shots brandy. Mix well and pour into bottle.

Olive Oil

What does "virgin" mean? It is the first pressing of the olives to make the oil. The first pressing is the strongest olive taste, and the most extra virgin. Later pressings are less virgin, until the last, which is light olive oil and not listed as virgin.

Extra virgin olive oil is good for sauces and dressings. Light olive oil is good for frying. The extra virgin oil can burn if used for frying.

Play Clay

(Vicki Meister)

1 cup flour, 1 cup water, 1 Tbsp. vegetable oil, 2 tsp. cream of tartar, 1 tsp. food coloring, ½ cup salt

Mix ingredients in saucepan and, stirring constantly, cook over low heat until mixture leaves sides of pan. Food coloring may be added to the water before mixing. Store in tightly closed plastic container.

Smelly Dishcloths

As a very young bride when I knew nothing about the kitchen, I always carefully rinsed out my dishcloth in hot water to "sterilize" it. In no time my dishcloth smelled awful. I learned from a more experienced cook that rinsing in *cold* water is the trick to keeping the dishcloth smelling sweet.

Spice Sachet

(Gloria) Makes a great small hostess gift, or tuck into your kitchen drawers or cupboards for a great spicy smell that lasts quite a while.

1 tsp. whole star anise, 5 tsp. whole cloves, 5 tsp. whole nutmeg, 6 tsp. whole ginger (I used crystallized ginger), 2 whole vanilla beans, 7 sticks of cinnamon, 1 Tbsp. whole allspice.

Mix all together and break up the beans and sticks and chunks with scissors or pliers so that pieces are smaller but not powdered.

Put a little scoop in a circle of pretty fabric, secure with a rubber band and tie with a ribbon. You can stretch the spices by adding about a ½ tsp. of dry rice to each packet. The rice absorbs the spice smells and bulks up the packets a little. I used a 9 inch circle (made a paper pattern using a wastebasket) and cut with a pinking shears. This recipe made about 8 sachets. This is not cheap—whole spices are very pricey and you want to use new/fresh spices for this, but it's fun and a nice little gift.

Edwards Brothers Malloy
Thorofare, NJ USA
October 24, 2013